The *House* of YOU

*Heart Hygiene
for Living
in a Dirty World*

Connie Bertelsen Young

WESTBOW
PRESS®
A DIVISION OF THOMAS NELSON
& ZONDERVAN

WestBow Press books may be ordered through
booksellers or by contacting:

WestBow Press
A Division of Thomas Nelson & Zondervan
1663 Liberty Drive
Bloomington, IN 47403
www.westbowpress.com
844-714-3454

ISBN: 978-1-6642-0605-2 (sc)
ISBN: 978-1-6642-0797-4 (e)

Print information available on the last page.

WestBow Press rev. date: 10/07/2020

Don't you realize that your body is the temple of the Holy Spirit, who lives in you and was given to you by God?

You do not belong to yourself, for God bought you with a high price. So you must honor God with your body.

(1 Corinthians 6:19-20 NLT)

Contents

Acknowledgements

I have been blessed to have wonderful people encouraging me with my writing. Since this encouragement began many years ago, even before anything I wrote was published, it would be impossible to recognize all of those who have influenced me. Nevertheless, I submit this short list of appreciation.

First, my husband, Dennis, who is always there in countless ways. Through his unusual love, patience and wittiness, he keeps me smiling and focused on what is important.

My pastor, Rev. Dan Zemlicka, has fanned my writing with inspiration through his messages and sermons. Also, he has repeatedly given me opportunities to creatively use the gifts that God has given me.

Rev. Michael White, who is my wise friend, author, publisher and minister. I'm most grateful to him for his repeated assistance with editing expertise.

Tim Sheehan, who generously opened the door of opportunity for me to write a column for two San Joaquin Valley newspapers. He will always be my favorite Managing Editor.

The following names are a few other friends whose words of encouragement and support came with perfect timing. With great fondness, I thank Sharon O'Brien, Anne Coffey, Yvonne Coley, Karen Denchfield, Georgia Owens, Darlene Severson, Bonnie Stephens, Sharon Tissue and Margaret Young.

Proem

I will be careful to lead a blameless life—when will you come to me? I will conduct the affairs of my house with a blameless heart (Psalm 101:2 NIV).

Every living soul has one. It's temporary, but it's your home for now. Pinch yourself. That's your abode, your very own "house." You've been there all your life. You know it very well. It's your body where your soul lives.

Probably sooner than you think, it will be worn out, and you'll want a better place to live, but like I said, it's only temporary. Someday soon, you'll be forced to move out. Everyone gets evicted, sooner or later.

The thing is, what you do with it now, and how you live in it, will make a huge difference in your next home, your eternal abode—and that one's *not* temporary.

I don't know about you, but I'm pretty happy that I won't have to live in this same old place forever. When you get my age, the repairs are limited, and sometimes the upkeep is overwhelming.

Perhaps like me, you look pretty average from the outside. Some residences are blessed with better looking exteriors than others, but when it's time to move out, it really doesn't matter much. You won't take it with you.

Meantime, while we live here, everyone's exterior

gets a few marks of age which shows up a little more each year from the weathering of life. The power sources can't handle as much as they used to; the walls seem to lose their sturdiness; the roof tends to get thinner; the sound system weakens; and the windows tend to fog up.

There are a few products which might help things look a little better on the outside, and the facade can hide a lot, but the interior, which has more significance, is generally hidden from view.

Your foundation[1] is really the most important thing. Without the right one, there's simply no hope. You have a choice in this. Remember to get it right, so you don't have eternal, structural difficulties.

Still, one can be assured that we'll all have a certain amount of trouble with our residence. For instance, it's very likely that a section of everyone's "house" gets some kind of damage from exposure, but that's the danger of having this type of architecture.

Those who choose see-through walls learn they are not unbreakable. Nevertheless, the Builder prefers transparency. Despite an owner's pretentious attempts, no part of any residence is ever hidden from His view anyway.

Like everyone's "house," your "house" is marvelously and intricately built, with amazingly unique details. The Builder is creative and purposeful, and He knew exactly what He made, even before your construction was complete.[2]

If you take the time to look carefully, you'll find that each of the "houses" around you have special potential within their miraculous design. However, homeowners need to comply with the Builder's specifications to enjoy the amazing possibilities. It's always best if the owner doesn't wait too long before those marvelous utilities become rusty from lack of use. Unfortunately, unused resources are all too common.

Clearly, every homeowner has a responsibility, and individual housekeeping choices will certainly, ultimately affect the extent of one's occupancy. Again, remember, this home is temporary. We will soon have a new dwelling.[3] So, please keep this in mind as you read the following pages.

Introduction

God, who made the world and everything in it, since He is Lord of heaven and earth, does not dwell in temples made with hands (Acts 17:24 NKJV).

"Cleanliness is next to Godliness." I remember hearing those words at a rather young age. I knew them even before the time I was old enough to read the little plaque on the wall in the small, country house where I grew up. After all these years, I can still see in my mind the painted, calligraphic letters on that handmade plaque.

I used to think those words were quoted from the Bible, but that's not where they originated, even though we can find many Bible verses related to cleanliness. That saying has been attributed to the famous theologian, John Wesley. He wrote, "Slovenliness is no part of religion. Cleanliness is indeed next to Godliness."[4] My mother thought he was quite right about that.

Mom was a persnickety, tidy housekeeper, and she expected her children to do their part to help keep our home clean, neat and organized—like making our beds every day, for instance. She knew there's a correlation between the condition of one's home and one's spiritual condition, too, and she thought one could learn quite a lot about a person simply by observing their housekeeping. Furthermore, she believed that if anyone's home was dirty, messy or disorganized, it was an awful disadvantage to those who lived there, and it would clearly be reflected in their lives.

It doesn't seem like many people are of the same persuasion about housekeeping nowadays. This is partly because the old school idea of a full time "homemaker" is almost non-existent. With both parents working, for example, there simply isn't opportunity to devote time to creating that heavenly, homey atmosphere and do those remarkable things which a different century of housewives tried to lavish on their families.

Few young homemakers can imagine doing things like cooking with what they could grow in the garden, making their own clothes, or baking homemade bread from scratch. In today's "disposable" society, most have no intention of spending their limited time ironing clothes or threading a needle to repair something.

I was interested in the results of a survey which a friend of mine did on Facebook. She asked people whether they bothered to make their bed every day. Surprisingly, most responders indicated they did not.

My grandmother would no doubt be appalled at this generation's indifference. Her routine involved bleaching the bedsheets, washing them in an old-fashioned wringer washing machine, hanging them on a clothesline to dry, and then ironing them before she most carefully made the beds with them.

Apparently, making one's bed is meaningless to many, and that, of itself, really doesn't matter much. I don't believe John Wesley was much interested in bed-making as he wrote his famous words. Still, unmade beds might be indicative of a careless inattention to which many have succumbed.

In the twenty-first century, lifestyles have understandably

developed differently for various reasons. Because of this, certain longstanding homemaking considerations have gone unheeded, disturbingly so, in some cases. Nevertheless, the homemaking I'm considering goes beyond keeping the dust off the furniture and producing those homemade baking smells emanating from the kitchen.

I hope that you'll see the point I'm trying to make by using negligent housekeeping examples for comparison with the untidiness of our hearts and lives. I think we all need to be more vigilant in the "housekeeping" of our soul.

Meanwhile, I want to be clear that although I think cleanliness is next to Godliness, even with our best efforts, we'll never attain immaculacy in our attempts for purity.[5] However, if you've noticed, the Lord seems to really like excellence. Yet, excellence isn't the same as perfectionism. I've learned that perfectionism leans towards self-righteousness and tends to mess with right priorities. Even so, since born-again Christians are the temple of the living God, cleanliness must be our quest.

Sometime before I considered writing a book on the subject, I began to collect scriptures that helped me identify some of the areas in my own life that needed "clean-up." My personal journaling always seems to be preliminary to the making of a book, and my logging of the following verses particularly inspired me with the topic.

I have been crucified with Christ and I no longer live, but Christ lives in me. The life I now live in the body, I live by faith in the Son of God, who loved me and gave himself for me (Galatians 2:20 NIV).

For we know that if the earthly tent we live in is destroyed, we have a building from God, an eternal house in heaven, not built by human hands (2 Corinthians 5:1 NIV).

We of the Church can always use a good Spring

cleaning—in *every* season. So, along with me, let's get busy preparing for the Guest who is coming soon. Let's turn on the Light, sweep the dirt out of our minds, scrub the grime off the floors of our hearts, throw out the spoils we've foolishly stored, organize the clutter, fill up the empty container, replenish our supplies, dust off our feet, and get going!

Connie Bertelsen Young

ONE

New Beginnings

I love fresh starts, and I'm grateful for each new day. I suppose it's a little weird, but when I have a goal to do something, I like to wait until the first of a month to begin, since a new calendar page seems to make it more distinctive. New Year's resolutions are important to me, too.

Whether it's deciding to go on a special diet, determining to quit a bad habit, joining an organization, trying a new exercise regimen, volunteering for something, learning a new skill, or something else, there are opportunities to begin again, to start over no matter where we are. The most wonderful beginning anyone could ever have is the new birth.[6]

For whatever is born of God overcomes the world. And this is the victory that has overcome the world—our faith (1 John 5:4 NKJV).

Being born again not only gives us a new beginning in the here and now, it promises a fabulous eternal life that will be better than anything we've ever experienced or imagined.

However, as it is written: "What no eye has seen, what no ear has heard, and what no human mind has conceived"—the things God has prepared for those who love him— (1 Corinthians 2:9 NIV).

Meanwhile, we press on, knowing that there will be a day when there will be no more tedious upkeep for living, because God will make all things new. (See Revelation 21:5.) We can look forward to living forever in a glorious place that God is preparing for us. Furthermore, it gives us purpose for the temporary exertion in this life.

Some people have no real purpose, and without God's direction, meaningless labor ends in drudgery and desperation. It's sad to learn about people who have lost hope, but for many of us, getting to the "end of our rope" or finding ourselves at the bottom made us want to choose differently than we did in the past. When things didn't work out the way we thought they would, we decided to choose a better way. Indeed, there are options.

Now listen! Today I am giving you a choice between life and death, between prosperity and disaster (Deuteronomy 30:15 NLT).

Our enemy, the devil, brings despair, and he will insinuate we have no choice. He always makes difficult situations feel like a dead end where we can't turn around, but the above verse makes it clear that Almighty God has given us choice—with the right choice leading to fulfillment and happiness, instead of hopelessness. If we entertain the devil's lies, we'll remain in misery, but the truth can set us free to change directions and enjoy new beginnings. Jesus gave us an important key for a new start. He indicated that each of us must change and become like a child.

And he said: "Truly I tell you, unless you change and become like little children, you will never enter the kingdom of heaven" (Matthew 18:3 NIV).

Change is necessary for new beginnings. Obviously, if

we keep starting over doing things the same old way, we won't experience anything new. You've heard the old adage, "If at first you don't succeed, try, try again." It may be more suitable to say, "If at first you don't succeed, try something different." Repeated trying without changing will not bring anything new.

We can have hope if we are teachable and willing to change. I've often said that human beings can be compared to plants. If plants don't change through growth and some kind of movement, however infinitesimal, they will shrivel and die.

I've indicated that I like new beginnings and change. One example in my life is that I've had 31 different residences in which I've made my home through the years. I actually enjoyed each move, but I don't think most people enjoy that kind of change. In this case, the change of addresses didn't count much when it comes to the new beginnings that I'm emphasizing in this chapter.

There are many kinds of necessary, life-transforming, new beginnings, but we don't usually like change when it takes us from our comfortable place and requires work. Again, just like plants, the alternative to changing is dying.

Tolstoy wisely said, "True life is lived when tiny changes occur."[7] Perhaps the alterations are miniscule, but they must be ongoing. If you take an hour, or even a day, and try to observe a plant growing, you won't see much movement. Human growth isn't very observable either.

I believe we all have a "growing edge," and our growing edge is more than likely the thing(s) we fear. Eleanor Roosevelt challenged us by sharing her secret about how to spur growth. She said, "Do one thing every day that scares you."[8]

Fear is common to all of us. Facing our fears and

embracing change can bring sparkle to a dull life. On the other hand, remaining passive and uninspired by anything new makes life as gloomy as a house with no windows. For an individual to take that first step in making changes, one must be inspired.

Without reward, motivation usually dwindles. People are motivated by different things. We may not be aware of what motivates us, but whatever it is, it reflects our priorities. It can be something we are passionate about. It might be status or recognition that motivates us. Trends can influence people. For some, it's the desire for acceptance by conforming to what everyone else is doing. The most common motivation is probably money. Others are motivated by things like pressure from others, philanthropic pursuits, fulfilling a fantasy, desiring to impress, to escape, to make an impact or supply a need. Boredom, pride, beliefs, guilt, compassion or love can motivate people also.

Examination of our personal motivations will expose our values and reveal a lot about ourselves. Jesus Christ spoke of how a high value for something can motivate a person.

The kingdom of heaven is like treasure hidden in a field. When a man found it, he hid it again, and then in his joy went and sold all he had and bought that field (Matthew 13:44 NIV).

You could say that the man in that parable "put all his eggs in one basket." That's not really the wisdom of the world in which we live, but it is divine wisdom when it comes to making Jesus our most valuable possession. Another way to put it in our twenty-first century vernacular is by saying, "I'm all in!"

Those who choose to totally surrender to Christ have found the true treasure. Through Him, they can have a fresh, clean, new beginning each day.

Heart Hygiene
Questions for
Chapter 1

1. Give some examples of possible "new beginnings."

2. What is something that motivates you?

3. Have you changed something in your lifestyle in the past five years?

4. Is there anything that you would like to change?

5. Identify something you fear (or once feared) which could be (or was) your "growing edge."

6. Read Matthew 6:33 and explain what this means to you.

7. Read Luke 18:27. Does this verse encourage you to make a new beginning?

TWO

Purity

When I was a little girl, our family lived in a little country town where almost everybody had a clothes-line in the back yard. I remember watching my mother washing our clothes and then carrying them outside to hang them on the line with clothespins. When I was tall enough to reach the clothesline, I helped her.

There was something especially fresh and good-smelling about the things that were dried in the breeze that way, but I suppose the air was cleaner back then. Nowadays, it's easier to stick a fabric softener sheet in the dryer to get a good smell.

The comparison point I want to make is the fact that there is a way to keep things pleasant and sweet smelling in the "house of you."

Live a life filled with love, following the example of Christ. He loved us and offered himself as a sacrifice for us, a pleasing aroma to God (Ephesians 5:2 NLT).

The Bible teaches us about an extraordinary wind that was stronger than the breeze that dried the laundry on that old-fashioned clothesline, and it changed lives forever.

When the Day of Pentecost had fully come, they were all with one accord in one place. And suddenly there came a sound from heaven, as of a rushing mighty wind, and it filled the whole house where they were sitting (Acts 2:1-2 NKJV).

The Holy Spirit was given first to the early gathering of the Church on Pentecost, but the refreshing touch of the Spirit is available to us today, also. He gives us hope and truth, purifying our lives.

It is by the blood of Jesus Christ that we are fully cleansed from our sin and made right with God (see 1 John 1:7), but we will face the battle of resisting odious sin as long as we live. Even when we do our best, our endeavors to keep ourselves pure can't be done without the help of the Spirit of God. To put it another way, without Him, we really stink!

I am the vine, you are the branches. He who abides in Me, and I in him, bears much fruit; for without Me you can do nothing (John 15:5 NKJV).

Those who rely on the Lord and pursue purity, will have abilities that can't be experienced otherwise. Living in His righteousness brings wisdom, knowledge and power into our lives.

The shepherd boy, David, faced the mighty giant, Goliath, with impressive confidence. Considering that the warriors of Israel were quite intimidated by this massive bully towering above the average man, we could wonder why young David wasn't scared to death. Later, in Psalm 71:5, David wrote where his bravery originated. Isaiah also told us where we can get confidence.

The fruit of that righteousness will be peace; its effect will be quietness and confidence forever (Isaiah 32:17 NIV).

That's a special promise. That verse indicates that righteousness will bring us peace. Who wouldn't want *quietness and confidence forever*? It doesn't just say *maybe*, but rather *will be*!

The famous writer, Alfred Lord Tennyson, understood the spiritual law of righteousness. He wrote, "My strength is as the strength of ten, because my heart is pure."[9]

The greatest men and women in this world have pure hearts. They aren't waylaid by guilt and fear from accomplishing great things. They understand the devil's basic tactics always pertain to impurity. If he can cause us to entertain sin and get a stronghold in our life, however "small," we will certainly be weakened and detoured from the path of success and fulfillment.

Should not your piety be your confidence and your blameless ways your hope? (*Job 4:6 NIV*).

Nowadays, we don't often hear the word *piety*. When we hear that someone is pious, we may be put-off with a connotation of self-righteousness, or someone seemingly hypocritically virtuous. The actual meaning of piety includes loyalty, duty to God, devotion and dutiful conduct. There isn't anything negative about that.

In this century, it appears that scrupulousness doesn't seem to be understood by many people in a positive way. In fact, individuals who are too meticulous about anything have been kidded or criticized as having OCD. Obsessive Compulsive Disorder is "a mental disorder in which you have thoughts (obsessions) and rituals (compulsions) over and over. They interfere with your life, but you cannot control or stop them."[10] It's a serious condition that shouldn't be besmirched in ignorant labeling, but the label certainly has been applied too loosely to people who simply want to set a high standard of excellence in what they do.

Instead of admiring those who conscientiously attempt to be very thorough in their endeavors, their fastidious ways are often insulted. With tongue in cheek, I'll suggest another label. This one is for those who are most likely to quickly criticize the more perfectionistic personality. How about LCD, which could signify "lazy, careless and disorganized"? *All* of us have a little of *that* in us.

Kidding aside, those who pursue the best that they can do are a blessing to a world that is haphazard about many things. I love the title of the great book "My Utmost for His Highest"[11] by Oswald Chambers. The title epitomizes what Christians should always try to do.

All of us who look forward to his Coming stay ready, with the glistening purity of Jesus' life as a model for our own (1 John 3:3 MSG).

After being born again and giving our lives to Christ, I think the most significant thing we can do to keep ourselves pure is to guard our thoughts. If we learn to simply change our minds when our thinking is wrong, we'll avoid a lot of muck.

My grandson finds it irresistible to purposely splash through mud puddles if they appear near his path to wherever he is going. This isn't unusual for children, but it makes it necessary to wash their clothes more often. In comparison, immature Christians can be careless in allowing impurities into their minds, making themselves dirty. Just like a parent will warn a son or daughter not to play in the mud when they are in their best clothes, the Holy Spirit will alert a child of God to keep out of the metaphorical mud puddles of life. Unfortunately, we are oftentimes careless and oblivious.

They are pure in their own eyes, but they are filthy and unwashed (Proverbs 30:12 NLT).

The Psalmist pleaded for God to give him a pure heart. (See Psalm 51:10.) He knew that he had to rely on the Lord for purity. Let us also ask God to create in us a pure heart.

Dear friends, now we are children of God, and what we will be has not yet been made known. But we know that when Christ appears, we shall be like him, for we shall see him as he is. All who have this hope in him purify themselves, just as he is pure (1 John 3:2-3 NIV).

Heart Hygiene
Questions for
Chapter 2

1. What is the essence of the aroma in Ephesians 5:2?

2. Read John 3:8. How is the wind compared to the Spirit of God in this case?

3. Why was David so bold in facing the giant, Goliath? (See 1 Samuel 17.)

4. Why was Eliab, David's oldest brother, so provoked by David? (1 Samuel 17:28)

5. How can piety increase your confidence? (Job 4:6)

6. How does Philippians 2:14-15 advise us to behave so that we may shine?

7. According to Matthew 5:8, who will see God?

THREE

Rags

We use rags for cleaning up things in our houses. We may scrub the floor with them, polish the furniture, make the mirrors shine, wash windows and use them to wipe up messes. The Bible compares rags to those things we try to do to make ourselves clean enough for God, but with all our scrubbing and polishing, we just can't clean up enough.

But we are all like an unclean thing, And all our righteousnesses are like filthy rags; We all fade as a leaf, and our iniquities, like the wind, Have taken us away (Isaiah 64:6 NKJV).

In the last chapter, the subject was purity. Salvation is a gift, and it must be worked out. (See Philippians 2:12.) Although we need to zealously pursue purity and righteousness, this chapter is a reminder that all our attempts at making our "house" clean enough by good works are futile. It may seem contradictory, but this is an important truth that believers must grasp.

Not by works of righteousness which we have done, but according to His mercy He saved us, through the washing of regeneration and renewing of the Holy Spirit (Titus 3:5 NKJV).

T.S. Eliot said, "It is not enough to understand what we

ought to be, unless we know what we are; and we do not understand what we are, unless we know what we ought to be."[12]

As it is written: "There is no one righteous, not even one" (Romans 3:10 NIV).

It is only through Jesus Christ that we are made acceptable to God. It is only through Jesus Christ that we can approach Almighty God. It is only through Jesus Christ that we are connected to God.

Years ago, I submitted myself to the Lord with my whole heart, and I was saved by His Grace. I determined to be "all in" as they say at my church. Yet, I was disturbed because the world continued to be distracting to me. Even the mundane tasks of my lifestyle took my mind away from concentration on Him, constantly pulling me away with one thing or another.

As a young Christian, I learned that "focus" is important and abiding in Jesus is mandatory. Keeping our minds on God is essential for peace. We must keep continually connected to the power source, but, oh, the distractions!

There are many things that can draw my heart and mind a million miles away. I wish I could say I don't get distracted any more, but that wouldn't be true. Nevertheless, I did learn something in those early years.

I really wanted to keep my connection to the Lord strong and consistent, even though the scripturally mandated idea of praying without ceasing bewildered me. I felt stumped in maintaining a regular connection.

It is so amazing the way the Holy Spirit works when we have sincere concerns. He began to give me answers. The first thing He put in my heart was, "It's not you who can keep the connection. You must trust that Jesus keeps you connected." Frankly, I thought, then why am I trying so hard?

Then I remembered one of the first Bible verses that I memorized after I was saved.

For I am confident of this very thing, that He who began a good work in you will perfect it until the day of Christ Jesus (Philippians 1:6 NASB).

I recognized the promise in that verse indicated that God will continue working in me all my life, despite my failures and poor attempts at being good enough. It said He was the one who began that good work, and He is the one who will continue it. After I digested that fact, I was reminded of another verse.

Truly I tell you, anyone who will not receive the kingdom of God like a little child will never enter it (Luke 18:17 NIV).

That verse made me think about how a helpless baby needs to be cared for by a parent, but comparing Almighty God to a parent, and myself to a baby, seemed like a tremendously understated analogy. The vast difference between who God is and who I am is incomprehensible and beyond comparison. Even so, to receive Him like a little child, despite my inability, fragility and immaturity, is the essence of what He wants me and all His children to do.

His stupendous love will keep us. Our responsibility is not to earn His love but to love Him and submit ourselves to Him in trust like a little child. He cares for us so deeply, beyond what we can think and feel, and *He gave His only Son.*

Before the Son of God took His last breath on the cross, He said, "*It is Finished*" (see John 19:30) so we can be forever connected with our Father. It has already been done.

For by grace you have been saved through faith, and that not of yourselves; it is the gift of God, not of works, lest anyone should boast (Ephesians 2:8-9 NKJV).

We've heard people say, "I'm a good person." They justify themselves by human evaluation, but Jesus made it clear that only God is "good." (See Mark 10:18.)

For all have sinned and fall short of the glory of God (Romans 3:23 NKJV).

Sadly, there are religious institutions that overlook the scriptural fact that Salvation is a gift and cannot be earned. They rely on being "good enough" instead of the Gift of God. They claim to believe in God, but the Bible says that even the demons believe in God. (See James 2:19.) Yet, we *know* that none of them will be in the eternal Kingdom of God.

I marvel that ye are so soon removed from him that called you into the grace of Christ unto another gospel: Which is not another; but there be some that trouble you, and would pervert the gospel of Christ. But though we, or an angel from heaven, preach any other gospel unto you than that which we have preached unto you, let him be accursed (Galatians 1:6-8 KJV).

The true Church will teach the fundamental truth regarding the Gift of God instead of works. Although there are many denominations scattered throughout the world, a Biblical test of doctrinal accuracy pertains to this Doctrine of Grace. It is a lie to believe that God will love us more because of our personal goodness, good deeds or achievements. Jesus Christ is our ALL IN ALL. We are utterly dependent on the generosity of God to save us by the blood of Jesus, to keep us connected to Himself, and to build our "house."

For every house has a builder, but the one who built everything is God (Hebrews 3:4 NLT).

Heart Hygiene
Questions for
Chapter 3

1. Read 1 John 1:7. Can we become perfectly clean?

2. What do you think is the difference between true righteousness and self-righteousness?

3. How can we be assured that we are clean and right with Almighty God? (See Hebrews 10:19 and John 15:3.)

4. Why should we pursue purity and righteousness? (See John 12:46 and Ephesians 5:8.)

5. Read Luke 11:33. Why should we share the Word?

6. For what reason did God send Jesus into the world? (See John 3:17.)

7. Read Romans 6:23. Why do you think there are some people who have never received the free Gift of God?

FOUR

Essentials

Most households have certain items which they think should always remain in supply to keep the residents happy. For instance, it might be items in the kitchen pantry, such as special seasonings, canned goods, ingredients for baking or ready-to-eat snacks. For me, those who know me can be *sure* that they will always find ice cream in my freezer. Naturally, everyone has different ideas about what is necessary to keep on hand, and if you ask around, you'll find people will have unique requirements.

There are many other things besides food that people consider essential to their comfort. Some wouldn't dream of living without things like a television, a particular musical instrument, books to read, a nice wardrobe, special tools or a computer.

I'm sure that you could add to these lists, and I could mention a lot of other things that people consider indispensable, but have you ever thought about what you would really need to survive? There are some interesting views on that subject, but let's look at what researchers agree upon. Scientists tell us that we must have at least four basic elements to live. These are water, air, food and light.

I happen to live in California, and as I write this book, water, the first element mentioned, has become much scarcer in this state. Because of lack of rain within the past few years, we've experienced drought, and we are forced to conserve water in every way that we can.

The second element, air, isn't what it used to be either because of recent wildfires. Also, other stuff that is polluting the air, coming primarily from factories and vehicles.

I think you might agree with me that some of the third element, food, has become a bit tainted, too, whether it is from various products used in farming, in manufacturing, or in the way food is preserved and prepared. Furthermore, we all know about fast food restaurants that offer tantalizing "junk food."

The last basic element that scientists say we need to live is light. Unfortunately, especially if we live in a big city or our work is indoors, the light to which we are exposed much of the time is coming from things like our lightbulbs, streetlamps, sunlamps, computers, laptops and televisions, but not so much from sunshine.

I wonder if these 21st Century exchanges, for what was once pure, basic, elements to help us live, are killing us. I don't want to get too negative, however. So, in this chapter, I want to concentrate on some different essentials for life.

Since our lives tend to get quickly "cluttered up" with stuff that isn't very important, especially the things that take up time and energy but are not satisfying, we need to figure out the basics. Longing for fulfillment, I have asked the Lord many times to "Show me how to live." One day, I finally heard His answer, but it wasn't really what I wanted to hear. He said, "First, I'll show you how to die." I wondered how death could bring life, but God wasn't talking about placing a tombstone over my lifeless bones. He wanted me to die to myself by surrendering my will to Him.

And those who are Christ's have crucified the flesh with its passions and desires (Galatians 5:24 NKJV).

I learned that the death of my fleshly ways was truly the beginning for what is essential to living a happy life. You could say I had a very personal funeral, between me and the Lord Jesus, so I could begin to live in Him. Christ is my essential for life.

For just as the Father raises the dead and gives them life, even so the Son gives life to whom he is pleased to give it. (John 5:21 NIV)

Despite my decision to die to my self-will, it continues to be a daily decision that I must make. I should also mention that the dissatisfaction that I sometimes experience can be an indication that I am pursuing things that are not meant for me to chase.

The root of our discontentment is usually due to wrong priorities. We can become deceived by grasping for things which we only *think* are important. Our lives can get muddled up with non-essentials, and eventually we become unsatisfied.

Those who live only to satisfy their own sinful nature will harvest decay and death from that sinful nature. But those who live to please the Spirit will harvest everlasting life from the Spirit (Galatians 6:8 NLT).

Our greedy human nature craves gratification, but it's a lie to believe that we will be gratified without seeking God first and putting Him above everything. Only He can fully satisfy us. When we submit our will and turn to the Lord for our choices, there will be peace in the "house."

You will keep him in perfect peace, Whose mind is stayed on You, Because he trusts in You (Isaiah 26:3 NKJV).

We tend to complicate life with what we think is necessary, or with what we think is expected of us, if we're not getting God's direction. We forget that simplicity is extremely important to having peace, but that's not what the world says, and sometimes, even the people who love us just don't understand.

People will always have opinions about how we should or shouldn't be involved in this or that. Peter, the disciple, loved Jesus, and yet one time he unknowingly tried to detour the Lord from His basic, essential purpose.

Jesus turned and said to Peter, "Get behind me, Satan! You are a stumbling block to me; you do not have in mind the concerns of God, but merely human concerns" (Matthew 16:23 NIV).

The big question is simply whether we are doing what God wants, or are we merely being self-indulgent and performing for people or for ourselves. That's a personal question that no one else can answer for us. People will look on outward appearances, but the Lord knows the truth and sees our hearts. (See 1 Samuel 16:7.)

It's easier said than done, but we can't worry about how others think we should live if we are choosing what God wants. Any other way but God's Way will be the wrong way, and if we go the wrong way, we'll carry too much. If things are getting too heavy, it's a sign that we aren't on target.

"For my yoke is easy and my burden light" (Matthew 11:30 NIV).

Generally, the more we take on, and the more stuff we acquire, the more the complications, responsibilities and housework! On the other hand, when the Son sets you free (see John 8:36), life become so much better.

"Do not lay up for yourselves treasures on earth, where moth

and rust destroy and where thieves break in and steal; but lay up for yourselves treasures in heaven, where neither moth nor rust destroys and where thieves do not break in and steal" (Matthew 6:19-20 NKJV).

Keep in mind that God didn't make "cookie cutter people." Each of us have unique purposes and strengths, making our endeavors diverse and our involvements and essentials necessarily dissimilar. Attempts at fitting the "mold" or comparing ourselves to each other will bring frustration. Furthermore, obligating anyone to act according to our limited assessments concerning their placement or calling, is wrong. We need to concentrate on our own housekeeping essentials.

The four basic elements which we need to live (water, air, food and light) can be compared to the more important spiritual essentials mentioned in the Bible.

Water: *The Spirit and the bride say, "Come!" And let the one who hears say, "Come!" Let the one who is thirsty come; and let the one who wishes take the free gift of the water of life (Revelation 22:17 NIV).*

Air: *And he is not served by human hands, as if he needed anything. Rather, he himself gives everyone life and breath and everything else (Acts 17:25 NIV).*

Food: *I am the bread of life (John 6:48 NKJV).*

Light: *Jesus spoke to the people once more and said, "I am the light of the world. If you follow me, you won't have to walk in darkness, because you will have the light that leads to life" (John 8:12 NLT).*

Jesus Christ is essential for life!

For in Him we live and move and have our being, as also some of your own poets have said, 'For we are also His offspring' (Acts 17:28 NKJV).

Heart Hygiene
Questions for
Chapter 4

1. What is something that you always consider essential for you to keep in your kitchen pantry or in your house?

2. If you could put only four items in a survival kit, what would they be?

3. What are some unessential things that bring enjoyment to your life?

4. Read John 6:48-51. Why is this bread essential?

5. Is there something that you think is "expected" of you that messes with God's Way for you or for better priorities?

6. What do you think Paul meant when he said, "I die daily"? See 1 Corinthians 15:31.

7. What does Romans 8:13 mean to you?

FIVE

Choices

*Who, then, are those who fear the **LORD**? He will instruct them in the ways they should choose (Psalm 25:12 NIV).*

We looked at what is essential in the last chapter, and with that in mind, it should help us to prioritize and make better choices for our "house."

This day I call the heavens and the earth as witnesses against you that I have set before you life and death, blessings and curses. Now choose life, so that you and your children may live (Deuteronomy 30:19 NIV).

The most important choice is clearly laid out for us. We can make the best choice by choosing life. It should be an easy choice to make. Why would anyone choose curses and death?

I choose life, and I suspect that you have also chosen life, or you probably wouldn't be reading this book. Nevertheless, we've all made bad decisions at one time or another. We are fragile people who are swayed by many things, yet we are required to keep choosing every day of our lives.

There's no way around it. This very day each of us has probably already made at least a hundred choices. For instance, we chose to get out of bed, what to wear, what we ate, the words we spoke, to whom we spoke, what we do with our time, where to sit, where we move, what we see and what we think. The choices we've already made today tell something about us. Hopefully, we will keep determining to choose what is right, because as one person said, "The hardest part isn't choosing, it's learning to live with the choice that you make."[13]

The Israelites spent 40 years in the desert with the choice they made. (See Joshua 5:6.) It could have been a much shorter journey, but apparently, they eventually learned from their mistakes, and they responded to Joshua's pleading for their obedience with the following decision.

The people answered, "We'd never forsake GOD! Never! We'd never leave GOD to worship other gods" (Joshua 24:16 MSG).

We all know how to talk big, and our intentions may be good, but when it comes down to "where the rubber meets the road," our choices may not be so great. Do you remember how adamantly Peter insisted about what he would do?

Peter said, "Lord, I am ready to go to prison with you, and even to die with you." But Jesus said, "Peter, let me tell you something. Before the rooster crows tomorrow morning, you will deny three times that you even know me" (Luke 22:33-34 NLT).

I wonder how Peter felt when the Lord responded the way He did to his enthusiasm. I don't think Peter really processed what He said very carefully, or maybe he wouldn't have messed up so badly. Like Peter, we've been warned about our weakness.

"Watch and pray, lest you enter into temptation. The spirit indeed is willing, but the flesh is weak" (Mark 14:38 NKJV).

We, too, have been zealous and made big promises. Nevertheless, we have all denied Jesus in our own way, and like Peter, it has been in our encounters with people.

Even if a servant girl hasn't asked us the same question asked of Peter, we have answered people with our prideful responses—or lack of response.

If our "housekeeping" choices are haphazard in the basic upkeep of watching and praying, that metaphorical rooster will eventually be crowing disturbingly. Thank God, when we *do* make the wrong choice, whatever it may be, we can be forgiven.

If we claim to be without sin, we deceive ourselves and the truth is not in us. If we confess our sins, he is faithful and just and will forgive us our sins and purify us from all unrighteousness (1 John 1:8-9 NIV).

We are all vulnerable, but as we grow in maturity and in obedience, we gain strength to resist sin. Still, we'll always have to make hard choices, and sometimes the answers are not obvious.

It can be very frustrating when the answer isn't clear–maybe even after we've prayed about it. Do you ever wish that God would speak a little louder?

I have learned that if I continue to seek God's will in matters, big and small, He will lead me, even when it's not clear. He does not give us all the answers, because He wants us to use our faith. Also, I believe it's the more mature child who is expected to wait.

And without faith it is impossible to please God, because anyone who comes to him must believe that he exists and that he rewards those who earnestly seek him (Hebrews 11:6 NIV).

When applying faith, I can be confident that all is well and everything is in God's hands. After I've submitted myself to the Lord and sought His direction concerning a matter, I can move forward. If the direction in which I'm proceeding is not His will, He will close the door or bring an obstacle to help me change my course. I've learned not to kick the door down. When the door is closed or some obstacle hinders access, I shouldn't proceed further until I look at alternatives and pray for understanding.

We read in the book of Acts that initially Paul didn't realize he was actually fighting against God by his self-righteous, religious endeavors.

And he said, "Who are You, Lord?" Then the Lord said, "I am Jesus, whom you are persecuting. It is hard for you to kick against the goads" (Acts 9:5 NKJV).

Sometimes we can't see that it's the Lord Himself who is responsible for delays or impediments that prevent us from moving on into something we want to do, or to some place we want to go. We may be on the wrong road because of poor choices, or it might just be the wrong timing, and God may thwart our advancing.

There's a great story in the Old Testament where God used a donkey that prevented a man from proceeding on a dangerous road. (See Numbers 23:21-31.) The Lord may use rather startling, metaphorical donkeys in our own lives to keep us from being slain by going the wrong way. Like Paul, we may be ardently choosing what we consider right, but we can't see the whole picture.

Cherie Hill wrote, "In your humanness, it is often difficult to realize your depravity."[14] We think we know a lot, but we don't see as much as we think we see.

Now we see things imperfectly, like puzzling reflections in a mirror, but then we will see everything with perfect clarity. All that I know now is partial and incomplete, but then I will know everything completely, just as God now knows me completely (1 Corinthians 13:12 NLT).

Our choices are certainly more complicated because of spiritual considerations and invisible things, but when God leads us, He will show us the correct way to go and deliver us from blindness. He opened Paul's eyes to things of spiritual importance on the Damascus Road, and Paul showed us from his experience to look at what is eternal.

While we do not look at the things which are seen, but at the things which are not seen. For the things which are seen are temporary, but the things which are not seen are eternal (2 Corinthians 4:18 NKJV).

Despite those times when we lack clarity, we mustn't throw up our hands and give up. God hasn't left us defenseless. He has provided important, basic guidelines for every choice we make.

He has shown you, O mortal, what is good. And what does the LORD require of you? To act justly and to love mercy and to walk humbly with your God (Micah 6:8 NIV).

Heart Hygiene
Questions for
Chapter 5

1. Give a few examples of choices you need to make every day, every week or every month.

2. How can you be forgiven for your bad choices? (See 1 John 1:8-9.)

3. Established priorities and goals are significant to making good choices. List at least two of your highest priorities and/or goals.

4. How does obeying the "most important commandment" affect all your choices (see Mark 12:28-30)?

5. Is there a choice you must make about something, but you feel uncertain about which way to go? (Read Proverbs 3:6.)

6. Have you experienced obstacles or closed doors in your life that you now see as God's hand?

7. Which is more important to you: what you *can see* with your eyes or what you *can't see*? Why?

SIX

Physical Maintenance

Every house, new and old, requires a certain amount of upkeep. It's the responsibility of the homeowner to keep things working properly. The Bible doesn't just teach about spiritual maintenance. Although it's the most important, and it certainly has bearing on our physical being, we are also instructed about specific considerations for our body.

May God himself, the God of peace, sanctify you through and through. May your spirit, soul and body be kept blameless at the coming of our Lord Jesus Christ (1 Thessalonians 5:23 NIV).

Those of us who are already "over the hill" don't particularly think of our bodies as "blameless." The point is, God cares about our bodies, and He wants us to do our best to take care of them and keep them in good condition as well as we are able.

The book of Leviticus shows some examples of specific remedies for things like skin diseases, discharges, postnatal needs and other bodily concerns of the Israelites. Of course, back then they couldn't search the Internet for medical information. However, these guidelines are just a few of many illustrations indicating that our physical body is important to the Lord. Meanwhile, especially for those of us who are "over the hill," we can look forward to the day when we will get a new body that won't ever need a cure.

And just as we have borne the image of the earthly man, so shall we bear the image of the heavenly man (1 Corinthians 15:49 NIV).

Until that day, we have explicit instructions for how we are to live in this temporary "house". God has shown us some rather unexpected ways for how we can be healthy.

Do not be wise in your own eyes; fear the LORD and shun evil. This will bring health to your body and nourishment to your bones (Proverbs 3:7-8 NIV).

According to that verse, the real key to health for the body isn't just diet, exercise and various prescriptions. Those things may be important, but the real keys are:

1. Not being wise in our own eyes
2. Fearing the Lord
3. Shunning evil

Health foods, tanning salons, and strenuous workouts at the gym can't compare with that promise for making us look good. Staying close to God and being in His presence through prayer and worship will literally make us glow with health.

Two examples of that healthy radiance can be found in Exodus 34:29-30, when Moses came down from Mount Sinai after speaking with God. Also, in Acts 6:15, Stephen was full of the Holy Spirit, and his face was like the face of an angel.

At the end of each year, many people, including me, determine to make New Year's resolutions for the improvement of their physical body, but we have a tendency to forget that our spiritual condition has profound influence upon this resolve. Perhaps that's the reason that Gallop polls show that so few people are successful in accomplishing their resolution goals.

If we are indeed saved, we have given ourselves—body, soul and spirit—to the Lordship of Christ. This means that everything we do with our "house" should be governed by Him. This includes eating, sleeping, working and playing.

And so, dear brothers and sisters, I plead with you to give your bodies to God because of all he has done for you. Let them be a living and holy sacrifice—the kind he will find acceptable. This is truly the way to worship him (Romans 12:1 NLT).

Often when the subject of stewardship is preached in the Church, it usually pertains to how we use our money for the work of the Lord. Yet, Biblical stewardship covers a broad spectrum.

Each of you should use whatever gift you have received to serve others, as faithful stewards of God's grace in its various forms (1 Peter 4:10 NIV).

Our human body is a gift of life that God has given us. We are required to be good stewards with our bodies.

Or do you not know that your body is the temple of the Holy Spirit who is in you, whom you have from God, and you are not your own? (1 Corinthians 6:19 NKJV).

So, since we belong to the Lord, we look to the Bible to see what He wants us to do and not to do with the body that He owns. For instance, there are multiple verses about how to use our eyes, ears, mouth, feet and hands. The following verse regarding our hands is only one example.

Anyone who has been stealing must steal no longer, but must work, doing something useful with their own hands, that they may have something to share with those in need (Ephesians 4:28 NIV).

We don't usually think of ourselves as thieves, but if we

aren't doing something useful with our hands and sharing with those in need, we need to make some changes. The Message version of Ephesians 4:28 asks, *"Don't you see that you can't live however you please, squandering what God paid such a high price for?"*

We can't do whatever we want in our eating, sleeping, working and playing if we are truly committed. That may be news to some Christians who only consider the spiritual side of life in Jesus, but as already noted, body, soul and spirit are all part of the temple "house."

I don't want to come across as being legalistic, but Jesus wants to set us free from being too self-conscious. If we are Christ-conscious, we will consider these things and listen to God's directions for our health.

Dear friend, I pray that you may enjoy good health and that all may go well for you, even as your soul is getting along well (3 John 1:2 NIV).

Again, our physical health is most relative to the health of our soul. Before we go further, though, it must be made clear that all people—righteous and unrighteous—will experience physical troubles at one time or another.

With our limited understanding, it is wrong to assume that every sickness, disease, or hardship is a result of personal sin or lack of faith. In fact, sometimes it's precisely for bringing glory to God. (See John 11:4.)

On the other hand, we might be reaping what we've sown. For instance, hatred and unforgiveness are the worst culprits in causing prolonged physical problems for individuals. However, love and forgiveness are the remedies.

There is always room for improvement for our health. If you haven't taken the best care of your body, it's not too late to begin now. Even if our New Year's resolutions failed, we have another chance at it. We can start over by first renewing our mind, and that will have a positive effect on the success of every other endeavor.

Do not conform to the pattern of this world, but be transformed by the renewing of your mind. Then you will be able to test and approve what God's will is—his good, pleasing and perfect will (Romans 12:2 NIV).

Transformation is possible for everyone, but continued, conscientious physical maintenance requires a lot of willpower. People who are successful in dieting, for example, are those who apply self-control. It's obvious that few of us have been diligent in restraint and disciplining ourselves in keeping our weight under perfect control. According to one statistic, 63.1% of adults in the U.S. are either overweight or obese.[15]

God wants us to be the best that we can be. As representatives of Christ, the unsaved will take note of our appearance, and our self-indulgence through overeating will not only affect their opinion, but will lead to our own poor performance. People are more likely to listen to those who reflect health.

. . . Each of you should learn to control your own body in a way that is holy and honorable . . . (1 Thessalonians 4:4 NIV).

Self-control is a part of the fruit of the Spirit that we have in Jesus. (See Galatians 5:22-23.) Victory over our bodies begins when we confess what God says, and there are no impossibilities with God. He never tells us to say, "It's too hard. I've been this way too long. I've tried before and nothing works for me. I can't do it." Is there something that God cannot change?

I'm also talking to myself when I say, "Be careful that you don't entertain the devil's lies regarding impossibilities. Be careful what you confess."

For we all stumble in many things. If anyone does not stumble in word, he is a perfect man, able also to bridle the whole body (James 3:2 NKJV).

Heart Hygiene
Questions for
Chapter 6

1. How would you rate your physical health (Poor, Average, Good, Exceptional)?

2. What changes could you make for more optimum health?

3. When it comes to eating, sleeping, working or playing, which of these things do you think you needs the most improvement?

4. In consideration of Ephesians 4:28, what is something useful you can do with your hands?

5. What things do you think could be the most likely to cause physical problems for you? (Examples: worry; difficult relationships; your job; unforgiveness; eating habits; your words; stress; lack of exercise; or other things.)

6. In what areas of your life would you like to exercise more self-control? (Examples: relationships; eating habits; working out; use of time; talking; thinking; studying; listening; or other areas.)

7. Read Mark 9:23. Is there something that you once thought was impossible that you now see differently?

SEVEN

Emotional Housekeeping

Helen Keller, an American author and educator who was blind and deaf from early childhood, credited her teacher, Anne Sullivan, when she wrote, "The best and most beautiful things in the world cannot be seen or even touched. They must be felt with the heart."[16]

Emotions are a natural instinctive response coming from our soul. Everyone has them. Eight basic emotions are: fear, joy, anger, sadness, disgust, surprise, contempt, and interest (or anticipation). They produce varied levels of intensity. Our emotions may produce sensations of excitement, ardor, unrest, tenderness, sentiment or passion, just to mention a few responses, and they can make us feel great–or not so great.

Sometimes our feelings make us feel too vulnerable and out of control. We may try to reel in our responses when they are too painful or when we want to hide our emotions. Although it's not always best to share or reveal everything we feel, psychologists tell us that suppressing or denying our emotions too much might cause them to come out in a different form, such as ulcers, headaches, digestive disorders or panic attacks. Also, investigations at the University of Rochester noticed that "People who suppress their emotions tend to have shorter life spans."[17]

Emotions are necessary, and we shouldn't be afraid of them. God knew what He was doing when He created man in His image.

For you created my inmost being; you knit me together in my mother's womb. I praise you because I am fearfully and wonderfully made; your works are wonderful, I know that full well. My frame was not hidden from you when I was made in the secret place, when I was woven together in the depths of the earth (Psalm 139:13-15 NIV).

In His humanity, Jesus Christ identified with us in experiencing human emotions. He wept (John 11:35). He was angry (Mark 3:5). He was sorrowful (Isaiah 53:4). He was zealous (John 2:17). He was disappointed (Matthew 26:40). He was anguished (Luke 22:44). He experienced love, joy, tiredness, pain, disgust, grief, hunger, contentment, despair and every human emotion. Yet, He was without sin.

It's dangerous to allow emotions to rule us. For instance, we may experience anger when we're provoked, but if we are vindictive, we've taken it too far. (See Ephesians 4:26.) We may experience grief, but it shouldn't be continual. (See Nehemiah 8:10 and 1 Thessalonians 4:13). The opposite— happiness—is like a drug for some people. If they're not feeling happy, they are absolutely miserable, and it's clear to everyone around them.

A fool vents all his feelings, But a wise man holds them back (Proverbs 29:11 NKJV).

Emotional displays are common in babies and children. Dramatic outbursts, however they are expressed, usually indicate immaturity, but we've seen them happen publicly in politics, the news, check-out lines, protests and demonstrations, meetings and varied confrontations with people of every age. Facebook and other social media sites also show many examples of those carelessly venting their feelings.

As I stated in the previous chapter, self-control is part of the fruit of the Spirit (see Galatians 5:22-23). As Christians, we have this special power available, so we don't have to behave like fools. Our feelings can make us vulnerable and take us off course if we allow them to lead us. Instead, we can use self-control and be led by the Word of God and our faith. The Apostle Paul showed the way to respond in all circumstances.

I know what it is to be in need, and I know what it is to have plenty. I have learned the secret of being content in any and every situation, whether well fed or hungry, whether living in plenty or in want. I can do all this through him who gives me strength (Philippians 4:12-13 NIV).

Serenity is a word that isn't used much anymore. Dictionary definitions of serenity include the quality or state of being serene, calm, peaceful and tranquil. A person who is serene is someone who has emotions under control. Nevertheless, serenity is not passivity. Christians who have that attribute still experience every emotion. However, they have a handle on their feelings because they know how to cast their care upon the Lord and draw near to God. Furthermore, they make God known by their calmness in all kinds of situations with that sweet spirit of peace reflecting the Lord.

It will help us if we can remember to identify when our emotional provocation is from the enemy. The devil attempts to control us with our ups and downs. Then we'll make poor choices. Have you ever neglected reading your Bible, or stayed home from church because you didn't "feel like doing it"? We know where those feelings originated.

So let God work his will in you. Yell a loud no to the Devil and watch him scamper (James 4:7 MSG).

Our response to the very first seconds of goading from the enemy is crucial! We must quickly consider the outcome of those thoughts that he puts in our mind and take control of them. Recognize that the battle is real and immediately choose to resist.

. . . above all, taking the shield of faith with which you will be able to quench all the fiery darts of the wicked one (Ephesians 6:16 NKJV).

Although there are congenital reasons that people have serious ongoing emotional problems, our emotional health is generally determined by two things. Although there are other things that could be listed, these two things are the most common overall.

First, it's **what we put into us**. We choose to entertain good or bad thoughts, which will inevitably lead us in our responses. Also, what we eat is quite significant. Whether we choose healthy or unhealthy food to consume, it might certainly affect the performance of our brain and body.

Secondly, and most importantly, it's **what comes out of us**. Specifically, the words and actions that come from us (which originated in our thoughts), whether good or bad, profoundly affect our emotional health. Jesus made it clear that what comes out of us is what really messes us up.

And He said, "What comes out of a man, that defiles a man. For from within, out of the heart of men, proceed evil thoughts, adulteries, fornications, murders, thefts, covetousness, wickedness, deceit, lewdness, an evil eye, blasphemy, pride, foolishness. All these evil things come from within and defile a man" (Mark 7:20-23 NKJV).

In chapter six, we learned that hatred and unforgiveness are the worst culprits in causing prolonged physical problems, but they also can cause exceptionally serious emotional problems. If we allow the poisonous seeds of bitterness to remain in our mind and hearts, we can expect that they will surely manifest and grow something harmful to the "house."

In Numbers 32:23 (NIV), Moses warned the Israelites that, ". . . *You may be sure that your sin will find you out.*" Invariably, all sin, whatever form it takes, has painful consequences. At times, our emotions hurt more than physical pain.

Although they are part of a healthy life, we simply can't depend upon our emotions and feelings. Sometimes our ignorance, or our denial concerning our own nature, keeps us from recognizing our great need for a Savior. Although we need to take responsibility for our responses, it is only through the grace and mercy of God that we survive our fleshly foolishness.

And my God shall supply all your need according to His riches in glory by Christ Jesus (Philippians 4:19 NKJV).

The bottom line is the fact that God is the one who meets our needs. At one time or another, however, instead of looking to the Lord to supply our need, most of us have mistakenly looked to a human being to supply it.

It may have been an emotional need which we thought could be satisfied by someone else's response. It can be very lonely when we feel like nobody understands how we feel. Expecting a mere person to meet whatever we think we need, emotionally or otherwise, can be very disappointing. If we don't receive from them what is desired, it will lead to things such as estranged relationships, animosity, divorce and unhappiness.

Again, imagining that a person, whether a friend, parent, spouse, neighbor, relative, boss, pastor, counselor, or any other human being to be the one who will rescue us and supply our needs, emotional or otherwise, is a mistake.

Looking up to our only Savior, is where we will find help. I've heard it rightly said, "Our help is vertical, not parallel," i.e., looking *up* to God, not *out* to people!

Hear me and answer me. My thoughts trouble me and I am distraught (Psalm 55:2 NIV).

Our thoughts can take us down to deep valleys of despair. At other times, we may have "mountaintop" experiences of euphoria. We may think we have bipolar disorder, but intense feelings don't make us abnormal. They're part of life. We can get a handle on them, and a key to that is making up our minds to trust the Lord and His supply.

But godliness with contentment is great gain. For we brought nothing into the world, and we can take nothing out of it. But if we have food and clothing, we will be content with that (1 Timothy 6:6-8 NIV).

Heart Hygiene
Questions for
Chapter 7

1. A common reason why our emotions get "out of control" is because we aren't getting what we want (see James 4:1). Consider something you want, and decide beforehand how you will respond if you don't get it.

2. Put a checkmark on the description(s) which best describe your emotional housekeeping? Often angry____ Bundle of nerves____ Controlled____ Fragile____ Healthy____ Expressive____ Tearful____ Hides emotions____ Vulnerable____ Fearful____ Excitable____ Reckless____ Stable____ Private____ Apathetic____ Responsive____ Free____ Balanced____ Passionate____ Uncontrolled____ Other?

3. Do you think bad feelings such as fear, hate, love or happiness can be contagious?

4. Since *what we put into us* and *what comes out of us* can provoke positive and negative emotions, name some good and bad things which may influence your feelings.

5. Do you think everyone should have someone to be a "sounding board" for their thoughts and feelings?

6. Name a person in your life with whom you think you could share your deepest feelings.

7. Read Ephesians 4:26. What does this verse mean to you?

EIGHT

Financial Upkeep

Don't run up debts, except for the huge debt of love you owe each other. When you love others, you complete what the law has been after all along (Romans 13:8 MSG).

We learn about money at an early age. Think of your childhood. Maybe it all began with the Tooth Fairy when you lost your first tooth. Many of us had piggy banks or a jar for saving coins. The kids in my family soon grew up preferring money for birthday and Christmas presents instead of other gifts. I know I did. That way I could buy what I wanted, and it wasn't always just clothes.

Money considerations are a part of our lives, and although our finances may not seem like a spiritual matter, our thinking about what money means to us and the use of it is very relevant. Like everything else in our lives, the Bible has something to say about the subject. So, to find good financial advice, let's turn to the scriptures.

The Word teaches us how we can prosper and be supplied with everything we need. We could pursue this subject by finding ways to increase our finances, since you probably wouldn't mind doing that. There are wonderful principles concerning becoming "rich," but don't get too excited, because the first concern in this chapter isn't how to accumulate more in the way you might be thinking about. Instead, the subject matter has to do with greed.

For the love of money is a root of all kinds of evil, for which some have strayed from the faith in their greediness, and pierced themselves through with many sorrows (1 Timothy 6:10 NKJV).

The above verse is misinterpreted by some who insinuate that *money is evil*. Rather, it is the *love of money* that becomes the problem, not money itself. I'm afraid most of us have been too obsessed with money at one time or another.

As an example, I recently spent a whole day trying to figure out which stores, online and local, were offering me the best deal for a certain purchase I had in mind. When I finally realized how distracted I was in pursuing this, it was too late, the day was over, and important considerations for my day were neglected. I rationalized that my intention was merely to be a good steward in spending, but in this instance, it was an unnecessary, irrational waste of time.

There isn't anything wrong with searching for the best purchase, but penny-pinching can be taken to the extreme when we find ourselves a little too fixated on "bargains." There are always more important considerations than that super sale, or those coupon for dollars off. Afterall, we are God's Children, and our Father owns it all.

The earth is the LORD'S, and all it contains, The world, and those who dwell in it (Psalm 24:1 NASB).

Materialism is a tool of Satan to distract us and change our focus. He wants us to develop a miserly, insatiable disposition. He'll try to make us greedy hoarders and to conglomerate our lives with heaps of stuff that we don't really need.

Hoarding is birthed in either covetousness or fear. It's

a grievous thing because it demonstrates lack of trust in God's provision. If we really believe God will provide for our needs, we won't waste time filling our homes with superfluous quantities of *things*.

Do not store up for yourselves treasures on earth, where moths and vermin destroy, and where thieves break in and steal. But store up for yourselves treasures in heaven, where moths and vermin do not destroy, and where thieves do not break in and steal. For where your treasure is, there your heart will be also (Matthew 6:19-21 NIV).

The world glorifies material things and money. The flesh shouts that ownership of certain things will give us favor, security, power, and comfort, among other things. However, those benefits come from the hand of God alone—when they are genuine. Although there may indeed be a type of gratification and usefulness in money and those super-duper items that the wealthy show off, wisdom teaches us something else.

"No one can serve two masters. Either you will hate the one and love the other, or you will be devoted to the one and despise the other. You cannot serve both God and money" (Luke 16:13 NIV).

You've heard it said, "You can't take it with you." From an eternal perspective, we recognize the triviality of those temporary worldly possessions. The assets that we have in this life are meaningless, unless we use them for good.

I tell you, use worldly wealth to gain friends for yourselves, so that when it is gone, you will be welcomed into eternal dwellings (Luke 16:9 NIV).

The love of money is a type of idol. The first commandment (Exodus 20:3) makes it clear that nothing should be in a place of importance above God. Besides, money and things could never compete or be better than having the Maker of Heaven and earth as our Father. Nothing is more prestigious, more powerful, or fulfilling than being a child of God. Again, it isn't money or things that are bad, it's when we place them above our love for God.

But put on the Lord Jesus Christ, and make no provision for the flesh, to fulfill its lusts (Romans 13:14 NKJV).

Plenty of research shows that material possessions really don't make us happier.[18] The things that give us the most happiness can't be held within our hands. Instead, true joy and fulfillment are derived from things like good relationships and spending time with those we love. They can be found in giving and doing for others, a job well done, and other experiences that make life enjoyable. The spirit of peace, love and thankfulness can't be bought, but it is available to the poorest and the richest person alike.

We need to be good stewards, but financial upkeep is really quite simple—if we trust the Lord to be our provider. We can choose to let Him manage our accounts. The "bank" of Heaven certainly has the best "interest rate."

As Christians, we have the potential to store up priceless treasures in Heaven. We also have the promise that we have an abundant life (see John 10:10) available to us in the here and now.

And God will generously provide all you need. Then you will always have everything you need and plenty left over to share with others. (2 Corinthians 9:8 NLT).

The Bible has a lot to say about sharing, and whether people share what they have received will rather accurately show if they really have faith in God. Furthermore, it will determine what they will ultimately receive.

Remember this: Whoever sows sparingly will also reap sparingly, and whoever sows generously will also reap generously (2 Corinthians 9:6 NIV).

For analogy's sake, try to imagine a full bowl of money that belongs to you to use however you wish. Beside that full bowl of money is an empty bowl. The empty bowl represents a need apart from your own needs. It could represent someone desperate for financial help, a missionary, a needy family, or any worthy cause requiring monetary assistance. Now, suppose you dump your bowl of money into the empty bowl to supply the need. The picture I want you to see is this. According to the following promise, your bowl will not remain empty.

Give, and it will be given to you: good measure, pressed down, shaken together, and running over will be put into your bosom. For with the same measure that you use, it will be measured back to you (Luke 6:38 NKJV).

Like Ambrose Bierce said, "Money: a blessing that is of no advantage to us excepting when we part with it."[19] It truly is better to give than to receive.[20]

Although I'm not a fan of "prosperity preaching," I do believe that God certainly rewards givers. Still, it seems our prayers to Him are usually about asking for things we want to obtain for ourselves, rather than asking Him to help us increase our giving.

God's economy principles are vastly different from the world's view of how we should use what we have. The heathen think that giving away what we have is illogical for ongoing wealth. To them, giving is a contradiction to receiving. The truth is there is no depletion in righteous giving, but the opposite is true of selfishness.

All of us are stewards, whether we like the title or not. The definition of a steward is a person who manages another's property or financial affairs and administers anything as the agent of another. Everything we have has been supplied by God who generously gives us what we need. His generosity is for the good of all, and our management is significant to our supply. If we refuse to share what He gives us, it will surely affect our blessing.

To those who use well what they are given, even more will be given, and they will have an abundance. But from those who do nothing, even what little they have will be taken away (Matthew 25:29 NLT).

As God's stewards, we have Biblical instruction as to how we can be effective with what He has given us. If we seek God first in every matter, we will surely be well supplied.

But seek first his kingdom and his righteousness, and all these things will be given to you as well (Matthew 6:33 NIV).

Let's seek Him first before we go to the bank, before we write the check, before we decide on a purchase, before we sell, before we spend, before we give, before we take. Indeed, let's seek Him first even before we get out of bed in the morning!

Now may He who supplies seed to the sower, and bread for food, supply and multiply the seed you have sown and increase the fruits of your righteousness (2 Corinthians 9:10 NKJV).

Heart Hygiene
Questions for
Chapter 8

1. Do you remember the very first way you earned money and why you wanted or needed money?

2. Read Mark 12:41-44. Why do you think Jesus was so appreciative of this woman, even though she gave much less than others?

3. List some examples of worldly wealth besides money (see Luke 16:11.)

4. Is there anything in your possession which you could give away because you aren't using it?

5. Name at least two material things that you own that you would rather not give up.

6. Is there a closet, a garage, or a room in your home overflowing and cluttered with too many things?

7. At this point in your life, check the description(s) which best describe your current financial and materialistic upkeep. Hopeful____, Cluttered____, Prospering____, Disturbing____, Philanthropic____, Miserly____, Good____, Cumbersome____, Organized____, Budget nightmare____, Better than ever____, Penny-pinching____, Lukewarm____, Terrifying____, Promising____, Constricted____, Improving____. Other?

NINE

Measuring Up

There's nobody living right, not even one, nobody who knows the score, nobody alert for God. They've all taken the wrong turn; they've all wandered down blind alleys. No one's living right; I can't find a single one. Their throats are gaping graves, their tongues slick as mudslides. Every word they speak is tinged with poison. They open their mouths and pollute the air. They race for the honor of sinner-of-the-year, litter the land with heartbreak and ruin, Don't know the first thing about living with others. They never give God the time of day (Romans 3:10-18 MSG).

Uh-oh. Those words leave no doubt. Did you get it? It might be helpful to read and study that passage in other Bible versions also, because I think we read those words in the book of Romans too casually.

It's easier to think of others in the wicked world around us as being the *"No one's living right,"* but it's a bitter truth to apply the scripture to ourselves, personally. We're all in the same boat. We don't measure up.

Despite pride and egotism in the world, somewhere deep down inside of us, we know we aren't perfect—even though we might try to hide behind a careful facade that disguises our fears and weakness. Nevertheless, have you ever wanted to go somewhere and hide when you were in the company of charming, confident and sophisticated people because you felt socially inept, awkward or klutzy? I'm so glad that Jesus came for losers.

Blessed are the poor in spirit, for theirs is the kingdom of heaven (Matthew 5:3 NIV).

Self-doubt has been a common malady of all time. Various experiences have contributed to poor self-esteem, but the fact remains that it causes many personal problems. Among other things, doubting ourselves can lead to difficulty in relationships, negativism, aimlessness and bad habits.

When we allow continued feelings of failure, guiltiness, or lack of confidence, our minds soon become cluttered, leaving no room for loving people. The Bible tells us to love others as we love ourselves, but if we are unable to receive God's love and forgive ourselves, we can't love and forgive others (see James 2:8). Again, the only love which you can really give is an overflowing of the love that you receive from God.

The root of those negative feelings indicates the lack of trust in God who offers His endless strength and love, even to the least of the least. Of course, no person is really "least" with the Lord. Through Him we measure up.

It may seem justified, considering we are such a mess, but disliking oneself is a terrible sin. God has an individual purpose and plan for each of us (see Jeremiah 29:11). No one is a mistake, and it is wrong to hate what God loves.

Neither height nor depth, nor anything else in all creation, will be able to separate us from the love of God that is in Christ Jesus our Lord (Romans 8:39 NIV).

There is an old saying that "Faults are thick where love is thin." Receiving the love that God has for us frees us from guilt, self-hate, and the inability to love others. It has an amazing effect on our lives. It helps us to stop expecting ourselves to be faultless and acceptable by our own ability. When at last we determine to depend on the perfection of Jesus to live in us, we are set free from the chains of inferiority and failure.

Although we are covered with His worthiness from the first moment we turn to the Lord, we need to remind ourselves of the truth when we fall back into self-reliance. Christians must daily repeat the process of humbling ourselves and relying on Christ as we did when we were first saved.

As for God, His way is perfect; The word of the LORD is proven; He is a shield to all who trust in Him (Psalm 18:30 NKJV).

Even though we can only really develop effectiveness and validity through Jesus, there's ruthless competition in this world that seems particularly important to those who measure themselves by their accomplishments. Some attempt to win superiority and gain self-worth that way. However, the craving for supremacy is often propelled by the feeling of inferiority.

Nowadays, I've noticed that awards are given to everyone competing, especially children, so that nobody will feel like a loser. This may not be wise, only because one must learn that nobody wins all the time, else expectations about life will be unrealistic. Notwithstanding, winners and losers remain rather well defined, and it seems we can't help comparing ourselves to each other.

Maybe it began with Nursery school when all our color crayon pictures were displayed by the teacher. We noticed our peers managed to stay within the lines a little better than we did. Wherever it started, comparing continues throughout our lives.

To list only a few things, we have compared grades, clothes, popularity, education, titles, bank accounts, residences and cars. Most of us want to "keep up with the Joneses." We may even compare our talents, skills, and giftedness, wishing we were more like someone else. Of course, that is foolish.

Each one should test their own actions. Then they can take pride in themselves alone, without comparing themselves to someone else (Galatians 6:4 NIV).

By making comparisons, we are, in a sense, denying the importance of our own uniqueness which God created in us. In the extreme, comparing can incite ugliness like jealousy, hatred and rivalry.

The devil has encouraged individuals to compare themselves to one another since The Fall. There are many stories such as the ones about Cain and Abel (Genesis 4:8), Joseph and his brothers (Acts 7:9), and Sarah and Hagar (Genesis 21:9) that show how comparing will lead to evil. It continued in the New Testament times with the Sadducees and Pharisees, Jews and the Gentiles, Greeks and Romans. It goes on in our churches nowadays, with many types of comparisons too many to list, with everything from the size of church membership to the comfort of sanctuary seating.

Looking at others to measure or define ourselves will not really help us. We can begin to do that only by looking in the mirror, and even then, we are quite blind. There is a way to learn our identity, however. A wise person said, "We can find out *who* we are by *whose* we are." As God's children, the source of our uniqueness and all our potential is found in our Savior.

Jesus said to him, "If you can believe, all things are possible to him who believes" (Mark 9:23 NKJV).

We have unlimited potential in Christ. Potential isn't

what we have done so far; it's what we are able to accomplish henceforth. In Jesus, it is more than we can imagine. Unless we do what we've never done, we won't grow and move into that potential.

We all have a "growing edge" that pertains to something new for us to move into. If we meet our growing edge by obedience and boldness, it will ultimately produce joy and fulfillment. Yet, the edge that God has created for us is not the same for everybody, which is another reason why we shouldn't compare ourselves to others.

The parable of the bags of money in Matthew 25:14-15, shows us that not everyone was assigned the same amount. It illustrates that people have the capability to do a lot with whatever they are given. Each of us can increase what he or she has received from God—if we are intentional and industrious.

But we have this treasure in earthen vessels, that the excellence of the power may be of God and not of us (2 Corinthians 4:7 NKJV).

God loves humble and contrite people (see Isaiah 66:2), but when we are unconfident and insecure, it produces self-absorption, not humility. In the past, I was deceived to think that anyone having a lot of confidence always indicated pride, but I learned that it was the source of one's confidence that mattered (see Proverbs 14:26). Being confident in the Lord means humility is involved. Jesus demonstrated it. Someone wisely said that to be humble is to have strength and power under control.

Instead of reaching for acceptance and approval from others, God's unconditional love relieves our insecurities. We have confidence in Him because of the assurance of His love. We do nothing to qualify for His amazing grace. It is a gift that makes us "measure up" through Jesus Christ.

The fruit of that righteousness will be peace; its effect will be quietness and confidence forever (Isaiah 32:17 NIV).

Heart Hygiene
Questions for
Chapter 9

1. What do you think is the difference between pride and confidence?

2. Unless you think you're perfect, list at least two things that you don't especially like about yourself. (Examples: I didn't graduate; I flunked math; I'm too critical; my life is boring; my nose is big; I hate my job; I'm impatient; or something else.)

3. Read Romans 8:31-32. Give an example and explain why a certain social situation might be or has been uncomfortable for you.

4. Have you ever felt inferior when you're with someone who seems to be a paragon of intelligence and confidence?

5. Can you think of a personal experience that caused you to doubt yourself or made you feel unworthy?

6. Have you honestly been able to receive the absolutely unconditional love of God for yourself—or do you still struggle with issues of where you've messed up or haven't been "good enough"?

7. Read Psalm 136:1-26. What four words are repeatedly emphasized in these verses?

TEN

Quality of Life

You prepare a table before me in the presence of my enemies; You have anointed my head with oil; my cup overflows (Psalm 23:5 NASB).

How do you measure quality of life? Some measure it by their physical health. It has been said, "If you have your health, you have everything." Others think it depends on how much money or things they have. For some, the quality of life is estimated in terms of relationships, work, purpose, peace, love and many other ways. The Bible, however, gives us the best gauge of real life.

He who has the Son has life; he who does not have the Son of God does not have life (1 John 5:12 NKJV).

That verse is starkly uncomplicated. It's like an arrow shot straight to the target of our souls, fearfully, wonderfully and straightforwardly true. We know that the basis for life is Jesus, and without Him, there is *no* quality of life—none, zip, nada, zero, non-existing, not a bit, not a whit, not a hint; **there is no life**.

I made my point. Thank God, there is LIFE—quality of life—through Him! By now, you probably see that this book was written to encourage every believer to do everything possible to live in that life while maintaining our "housing." We can only do that by following Christ.

Jesus told his disciples that they would know the way to follow Him, but Thomas didn't understand what Jesus was saying until the Lord elaborated. John's Gospel states:

Jesus told him, "I am the way, the truth, and the life. No one can come to the Father except through me" (John 14:6 NLT).

You might remember that the Samaritan woman at the well also needed some elaboration concerning what Jesus was suggesting. She didn't understand how anything could quench her thirst eternally, but she wanted it.

"Anyone who drinks the water I give will never thirst—not ever. The water I give will be an artesian spring within, gushing fountains of endless life" (John 4:14 MSG).

In our longing for a fulfilling life, we can identify with that Samaritan woman who wanted her thirst quenched. Still, in our desire for satisfaction, we may turn to worldly things, but when we do, we soon find ourselves thirsty again. The book of Isaiah reminds us that we are wasting our time trying to find gratification in fleshly things.

"Is anyone thirsty? Come and drink—even if you have no money! Come, take your choice of wine or milk—it's all free! Why spend your money on food that does not give you strength? Why pay for food that does you no good? Listen to me, and you will eat what is good. You will enjoy the finest food" (Isaiah 55:1-2 NLT).

The world today has a lot of advantages which weren't available in Isaiah's day. The Word of God has always been and will always be our most important possession, but now we have amazing technology, science and medical knowledge. We have information which can help us live exemplary lives.

There are things that we now know to do in order to

experience more well-being and enjoy a longer life. For instance, diabetics must watch their sugar intake; heart patients are told to avoid fatty foods; and everyone is encouraged to exercise, eat healthfully and stop smoking. Surprisingly, some people refuse to change their habits, even though indulging in certain things will bring them problems.

I overheard a discussion between a caregiver and a terminally ill individual. The physician had insisted that the patient needed bed rest and was certainly not to venture outdoors. Ignoring the doctor's orders, the patient defiantly got out of bed and proceeded to leave the house as soon as the doctor left the room. The concerned caregiver asked the person why he would not stay in bed. The patient answered, "I will do exactly what I want to do in the remaining days of my life. I would rather die while I'm taking a walk in my garden, enjoying the flowers that I love, than to die in my bed in this bleak room." It was clear that the quality of life was more important to that person than a long life, and there's something to be said for that viewpoint.

Technically, we all have a "terminal diagnosis." It's a shame for anyone to wait until the end is near before living life to the fullest. We tend to forget that we aren't invincible. This life will certainly end for each of us, although we don't know the day. If we knew that we had only one month to live, I think most of us would probably make some changes.

Everyone has to die once, then face the consequences (Hebrews 9:27 MSG).

The movie, *The Bucket List*, is about two unlikely friends with incurable illnesses. When sharing a hospital room, they determine to get out and do the things they always wanted to do before they die. Ultimately, in doing this, they find great friendship and joy in living.

In another movie, *The Last Holiday*, a woman is given an incorrect diagnosis by her doctor. Thinking that she might die soon, she decides to go "all in" using all her resources to have a fabulous vacation that she always dreamed of having. When at last she discovers that her diagnosis was incorrect, she'd already experienced the freedom of jubilant living without inhibition, and she was never the same again.

As Christians who are "all in," we can experience delightfully extravagant lives in Jesus. The extravagance we experience is the fabulous joy that God gives when we are fully committed to Him. This is better than any luxurious, worldly vacation.

A thief is only there to steal and kill and destroy. I came so they can have real and eternal life, more and better life than they ever dreamed of (John 10:10 MSG).

Scripture repeatedly shows us how to live a quality life. Life in Christ and obedience to Him not only gives us "joie de vivre"[21], it can also extend our life. Even children have been given a promise for an extended life when they obey the Word. (See Ephesians 6:1-3).

I call heaven and earth to witness against you today, that I have set before you life and death, the blessing and the curse. So choose life in order that you may live, you and your descendants (Deuteronomy 30:19 NASB).

A quality life is available to people of every age. A particularly important secret for experiencing that life is simply gratitude. The measure of our thankfulness affects the amount of our contentment. Rachel Cruze said, "In a heart filled with gratitude, there is no room for discontentment."[22]

You can test this theory the next time you feel discontented. Spend a few minutes thanking the Lord for His goodness. It might help you to get in the spirit of thanksgiving by making a list of some of the things you appreciate.

I believe that you'll find an attitude of sincere thankfulness generates joy. However, when we feel deprived in one way or another (which is insinuating that God hasn't supplied our need), feelings of resentment will rob us of fulfillment. A complaining attitude smothers quality of life.

Let them sacrifice the sacrifices of thanksgiving, And declare His works with rejoicing (Psalm 107:22 NKJV).

Perhaps you've heard the phrase, "This is as good as it gets." I don't appreciate those words because they imply there is nothing better. The Bible promises something extraordinarily better. We may try to measure our lives by what we experience and what we see, but there is so much more.

But as it is written: "Eye has not seen, nor ear heard, Nor have entered into the heart of man The things which God has prepared for those who love Him" (1 Corinthians 2:9 NKJV).

Our perspective on the quality of life is generally limited to what we have seen and heard with our eyes and ears. Someday soon, those who love the Lord will be filled up to the brim with the full measure of life, and our salvation will be complete!

Till we all come to the unity of the faith and of the knowledge of the Son of God, to a perfect man, to the measure of the stature of the fullness of Christ (Ephesians 4:13 NKJV).

Heart Hygiene
Questions for
Chapter 10

1. According to 1 Timothy 6:18-19, how do we take hold of real life?

2. Name at least two things that have brought quality to your life. (Examples: relationships, use of time, decisions, purpose, health considerations, job, etc.)

3. Jesus indicated that He will return when we don't expect Him. (Matthew 24:44). What would you do or what changes would you make to prepare if you knew He was coming in one week?

4. If you have a "Bucket List," list at least one of your goals.

5. On a scale of 1-10, with ten being the highest quality life and one being the lowest, how would you rate your life today? Is your rating better than five years ago?

6. In John 10:10, we learn that Jesus came to give us an abundant life. List at least three things that He has generously given to you.

7. Write a short prayer of thanksgiving.

ELEVEN

Repentance

I prefer not to use air fresheners, mainly because they don't get the job done. Generally, their purpose is covering the odor of something that is dirty or unpleasant. They hide the problem instead of taking care of it. Sooner or later, the cover-up stops working. Usually, a good scrubbing is the only thing that will rid bad smells. I've never found an air freshener that smells as nice as the scent of a freshly cleaned room.

There is no quick-fix cover-up that keeps the "house" of our souls clean and fresh either. We may mask our face with a smile and say religious words that sound good, but there is only one remedy to make us clean, and without it, the filth remains. It is only through faith in the blood of Jesus that we can be cleansed from our sins.

This is the message we have heard from Him and announce to you, that God is Light, and in Him there is no darkness at all. If we say that we have fellowship with Him and yet walk in the darkness, we lie and do not practice the truth; but if we walk in the Light as He Himself is in the Light, we have fellowship with one another, and the blood of Jesus His Son cleanses us from all sin (1 John 1:5-7 NASB).

We need repeated cleaning, just like our houses need repeated cleaning. A few years ago, when my husband and I moved into our current residence, the house had been thoroughly cleaned for new occupancy, but it wasn't long before the dust and grime began to accumulate after our move, just from normal living. If we hadn't kept up with regular cleaning, our home would be terribly dirty now. It would be repulsive to live in a house that's never cleaned.

In comparison, sin wrecks the quality of our body, soul and spirit life and makes us miserable. As noted in chapter ten, merely existing without quality isn't worth much. Repentance is a basic need for every believer in order to have a fulfilling and victorious existence.

As Christians, since we know that God has forgiven us of our sins and given us hope that we will spend eternity in Heaven with Him, we may become too complacent or haphazard in dealing with daily sin. That's a big mistake.

Sincere repentance always follows the genuine salvation experience. We are brought to an acute conviction of sin immediately prior to receiving Jesus as our Savior, but penitence doesn't end once we are born again. We are told to continue to "work out our salvation" (Philippians 2:12).

The need for repentance is mentioned repeatedly throughout this study. No, we can't be perfect, but the necessity for us to keep clean can't be overstated. Not only will unconfessed sin make us miserable, it will make us ineffective in sharing our faith. Furthermore, contrition accomplishes wonderful things that our enemy wants us to overlook. First of all, repentance frees us from the dominion of evil.

And having been set free from sin, you became slaves of righteousness (Romans 6:18 NKJV).

Repentance brings revival—both to individuals and to the Church. Not only do we experience individual refreshment, our personal repentance influences the health of the entire Church. This is because every single member of the Body of Christ affects the well-being of the whole Body.

Keeping clean is a profound responsibility for every Christian. The state of each of our hearts and minds will certainly bring negative or positive implications to our fellowship. To take it a huge step further, the Body of Christ impacts the state of the world.

Repent, then, and turn to God, so that your sins may be wiped out, that times of refreshing may come from the Lord, and that he may send the Messiah, who has been appointed for you—even Jesus (Acts 3:19-20 NIV).

We can realize how important repentance is for our health and stability, but we must first be aware of what exactly it is for which we need to repent, so that we can change our ways. Would you agree that it's usually easier to see the sin of other people than to identify our own?

Search me, God, and know my heart; test me and know my anxious thoughts (Psalm 139:23 NIV).

With a humble attitude recognizing our inborn propensity to sin, we can ask the Lord to show us the specifics, even when we may think we already know. You may have noticed that the Lord favors those that are humble (see Isaiah 57:15, Proverbs 3:34, James 4:6, and 1 Peter 5:5). We will experience a powerful presence of the Spirit following our genuine repentance. The Holy Spirit draws us into a more intimate relationship.

I keep asking that the God of our Lord Jesus Christ, the

glorious Father, may give you the Spirit of wisdom and revelation, so that you may know him better (Ephesians 1:17 NIV).

The central point is that we may know Him better. Honest repentance is not sought just to achieve our own dazzling spotlessness, but rather we are choosing to turn away from wickedness because we don't want whatever foul thing that is in us to keep us from drawing nearer to the Lord Jesus.

There is an intrinsic longing within us to know God, and it's a desire that cannot be satisfied until it is filled with Him. If we genuinely crave this, we will determine to repent of our sin. Repentance follows when we're convicted of transgression and acknowledge that it separates us from the righteousness of God.

Purify me from my sins, and I will be clean; wash me, and I will be whiter than snow (Psalm 51:7 NLT).

Imagine what peace and rest we could have in the world and in our relationships if we were always willing to admit our sin and repent quickly. Sadly, we often carelessly delay repenting, believing the demonic lie that a little "stain" doesn't matter and there's no urgency to ask for forgiveness. Jesus taught us the need of being faithful in everything, even in what we think are small things. All sin separates us from God—and that is *never* a small thing.

This is what the Sovereign LORD, the Holy One of Israel, says: "In repentance and rest is your salvation, in quietness and trust is your strength, but you would have none of it" (Isaiah 30:15 NIV).

There are often spiritual strongholds of evil that must be overcome in order to experience that rest. Things that get in the way of sincere repentance include pride, hypocrisy, blindness to guilt, wrong priorities, indifference, distraction, unaccountability and refusal to admit sin. Even as Christians, we have been guilty of each of those things.

In the past God overlooked such ignorance, but now he commands all people everywhere to repent (Acts 17:30 NIV).

The first step is surrendering to Christ and determining to seek Him above everything, every day (see Matthew 6:33 and Jeremiah 29:13). Then, when we sin, we have forgiveness and are washed and covered by the cleansing blood of Jesus.[23]

If we say that we have no sin, we deceive ourselves, and the truth is not in us. If we confess our sins, He is faithful and just to forgive us our sins and to cleanse us from all unrighteousness. If we say that we have not sinned, we make Him a liar, and His word is not in us (1 John 1:8-10 NKJV).

We will be in great danger if we allow ourselves to become smug in a counterfeit religious tranquility. Keeping a contrite heart and acknowledging our own sins is primary, although we often point fingers at the heathen and express our disdain for their misconduct. It would be better if we looked in the mirror to acknowledge our own need for correction. Surely, God is calling His very own people to repent of their wrongdoings, again and again.

If my people, who are called by my name, will humble themselves and pray and seek my face and turn from their wicked ways, then I will hear from heaven, and I will forgive their sin and will heal their land (2 Chronicles 7:14 NIV).

Heart Hygiene
Questions for
Chapter 11

1. Read Isaiah 66:1-2. According to this scripture, who are the ones that the Lord looks on with favor?

2. Sin separates us from God. Read Ephesians 2:13 and tell what can make anyone right with God.

3. Read Philippians 2:12 and explain how you can do this.

4. In your own words, what does repentance mean to you?

5. Has there been something specific in your conduct recently for which you have been truly sorry?

6. Using one or two sentences, write a simple prayer expressing your sorrow and regret for your sin.

7. Tell of a personal experience when you knew you were washed and forgiven.

TWELVE

Hospitality

Do not forget to show hospitality to strangers, for by so doing
some people have shown hospitality to angels without knowing it
(Hebrews 13:2 NIV).

Have you ever wondered if you have seen an angel? I
knew a couple of friends whom I suspected were angels, but
I guess I'll never know. Still, even when we aren't aware of
angelic presence, they are surely around us. (See Hebrews
1:14 and Psalm 91:11.)

Perhaps we should consider that every stranger we
meet could be an angel. It might make us a little more
conscientious about practicing hospitality.

I used to think that showing hospitality meant cooking
a special meal and setting the table for company like my
mother used to do when I was a child. I know she had the
gift of hospitality. When friends came for dinner, the long
table in the dining room looked perfect, with shining plates,
glasses, silverware and napkins, each in the right place. A
bouquet of flowers or a special centerpiece was placed in the
middle of the elegant setting, and maybe even candles on
each end of the table for ambiance. When her guests all sat

down in their designated places, and after my dad prayed a prayer of thanks to the Lord for the meal, Mother passed out bowls and platters of unforgettable, delicious homemade food.

I remember all the major preparations that seemed to be required, and how worn-out my mom was, even before the guests arrived. So, frankly, my idea of hospitality was something that I didn't particularly want to be too involved in. Eventually, I learned I was looking at the word very narrowly, and I needed to see what it meant to be hospitable.

According to *Webster's Dictionary*, the definition of hospitable includes friendly; kind; solicitous to a guest; receptive; and favoring the health, growth, and comfort of new arrivals.[24]

Having hospitality doesn't mean preparing an extravagant banquet like my mother used to do for people. I can be hospitable in ordinary situations. It may be as easy as being patient with the over-worked clerk at the grocery store, waving at people in my neighborhood as they walk or drive by my home, and answering the doorbell with a smile, even though I may not want to buy the product that the solicitors are selling.

Be hospitable to one another without grumbling (1 Peter 4:9 NKJV).

Experiencing community is necessary to a healthy life, and hospitality is an attribute. Obviously, if there is no social life, hospitality isn't a factor, but for whatever reason someone may have for continuing to isolate themselves from people, they will experience a cold environment.

Many of us experienced that "coldness" during the Corona Virus pandemic. For the first time in our lives, our interaction with people became terribly limited. I think we became more appreciative of hospitality through this experience!

Hospitality sparks warmth, bringing love and comfort. Everyone needs contact with people for health. Even if this technological world makes it possible to insulate ourselves from each other so we don't have face-to-face communications, it is not advisable to withdraw from all personal interaction. We will not thrive in isolation. John Donne wisely said, "No man is an island . . .."[25]

For none of us lives to himself, and no one dies to himself (Romans 14:7 NKJV).

The epitome of loneliness is the lack of contact with people. Also, self-centeredness is a big reason that people become lonely. Hospitality is a remedy for loneliness through reaching out to others in friendliness. Sometimes we are hesitant to reach out to people, particularly people that we don't know. Nonetheless, there will be a great reward for those who do.

And He will set the sheep on His right hand, but the goats on the left. Then the King will say to those on His right hand, 'Come, you blessed of My Father, inherit the kingdom prepared for you from the foundation of the world: for I was hungry and you gave Me food; I was thirsty and you gave Me drink; I was a stranger and you took Me in' (Matthew 25:33-35 NKJV).

Gillian Sandstrom, psychologist and university lecturer, said, "People feel more connected when they talk to strangers, like they are part of something bigger."[26] On the other hand, without the feeling of acceptance and connection, a person may feel detached and inferior. We are well advised to show kindness to strangers.

I have no greater joy than this, to hear of my children walking in the truth. Beloved, you are acting faithfully in whatever you accomplish for the brethren, and especially when they are strangers (3 John 1:4-5 NASB).

If you have ever been in a situation, such as your first visit to a church filled with people you didn't know, you might understand (and, hopefully, have experienced) the comfort of hospitality. Hospitality is vital for the Church, and God's people have always been encouraged to be hospitable.

The stranger who dwells among you shall be to you as one born among you, and you shall love him as yourself; for you were strangers in the land of Egypt: I am the LORD your God (Leviticus 19:34 NKJV).

The basic aspect of hospitality pertains to sharing—and it comes in many forms. Maybe you prefer the elaborate setting that my mother liked, but it could also be at a card table with paper plates and pizza. Also, hospitable sharing may be monetary, like when you support the missionary who needs your help, or when you drop money into the Salvation Army bell ringer's basket.

We ought therefore to show hospitality to such people so that we may work together for the truth (3 John 1:8 NIV).

After difficulties in a ship at sea, Paul and his shipmates were stranded on the island of Malta. In Acts 28:7, Luke told us of a chief official who welcomed Paul and those with Paul to his home and showed *generous hospitality.* Although they were strangers to him, they were able to stay at his estate for three days.

The essence of hospitality is love and sharing your love with people. It's removing the "Do not disturb" sign and opening the "door" to the "house of you" in unselfishness and bigheartedness.

So let's not get tired of doing what is good. At just the right time we will reap a harvest of blessing if we don't give up. Therefore, whenever we have the opportunity, we should do good to everyone—especially to those in the family of faith (Galatians 6:9-10 NLT).

Heart Hygiene
Questions for
Chapter 12

1. What is a way you could be hospitable to strangers in a grocery store?

2. Have you ever encountered a stranger that you thought might have been an angel?

3. List three different ways you could share a meal with a needy person.

4. Explain how you responded in the past when a total stranger reached out to you.

5. How could you show hospitality with your vehicle?

6. Describe how someone's hospitality to you has affected your life.

7. Underline the statement(s) which best describe you: I always show hospitality to strangers; I don't usually acknowledge strangers; I try to make new people feel welcomed; I have used my home for entertaining more than family; I'm uncomfortable being with people I don't know; I don't fellowship with Christians except at church; I need to ask the Lord to help me to be hospitable.

THIRTEEN

Repairs

Wake up! Strengthen what remains and is about to die, for I have found your deeds unfinished in the sight of my God (Revelation 3:2 NIV).

As mentioned in Chapter One, I've lived in a lot of different residences, some of them were new and some of them old, but sooner or later, some kind of reparation was needed in all of them, even in the newer homes. It's just a matter of time before the things that *moth and rust destroy* (see Matthew 6:19-20) seem to breakdown, wear out or deteriorate in time. As a homeowner, keeping up with repairs is necessary so that one's residence will not become uninhabitable.

The "house of you" will require regular repairs to keep you from early dilapidation. Sometimes it's physical, but probably more often it's our soul that needs mending. Until we get our divine new home, which won't need repairing, we will get weatherworn areas that need repeated fixing.

I am feeble and sore broken: I have roared by reason of the disquietness of my heart (Psalm 38:8 KJV).

The probable damage we'll experience at one time or

another include broken hearts, sickness, discouragement, selfishness, guilt and various infestations in our minds. Of course, that's only a piddling few of the many areas that require our continued attention. There are many things that steal our attention and affection from God, and the people of God have needed fixing since Adam and Eve.

Jesus Christ was the only man ever to live on earth who was always perfect. He had a "house" similar to the "house of you" and He described himself as a temple.

Jesus answered and said to them, "Destroy this temple, and in three days I will raise it up." Then the Jews said, "It has taken forty-six years to build this temple, and will You raise it up in three days?" But He was speaking of the temple of His body (John 2:19-21 NKJV).

Our bodies are the temple of the Holy Spirit (see 1 Corinthians 6:19-20). So, for comparison's sake, let's look in the fifth chapter of 1 Kings to see another kind of temple that was built.

Although this temple was man-made, it was to be the temple of the Lord. King Solomon was responsible for the first building of this glorious, extravagant building, with every detail stipulated by God Himself.

"Behold, I intend to build a house for the name of the LORD my God, as the LORD spoke to David my father, saying, 'Your son, whom I will set on your throne in your place, he will build the house for My name'" (1 Kings 5:5 NASB).

Like the "house of you", that temple was precisely and intricately made. It was a place created for worshiping the Lord, and it housed the Glory of God. The way the temple was built was according to specific instructions from God. Does that sound familiar?

The nation of Israel and every child of God have been given detailed guidelines for the house that was created for the dwelling of God. Every feature of the temple that King Solomon was to build was specified, but in our case, I think I could say we have a holy "repair book for dummies", because we have the Bible. It contains step by step instructions, and it's really not difficult to understand what we need to do.

"For precept must be upon precept, precept upon precept, Line upon line, line upon line, Here a little, there a little" (Isaiah 28:10 NKJV).

Meanwhile, we grow in learning, and as we gain wisdom and knowledge, we make needed renovations. Haggai expressed the need for repair in the following passage. Certainly, it could be applied to our society also.

"Is it time for you yourselves to dwell in your paneled houses, and this temple to lie in ruins?" (Haggai 1:4 NKJV).

We may be putting too much emphasis on our worldly residences and material things and neglecting the temple of the Holy Spirit. As always, our priorities reflect the realness of our faith, and until our priorities are right, whatever repairs we have in mind won't work.

"But everyone who hears these words of mine and does not put them into practice is like a foolish man who built his house on sand. The rain came down, the streams rose, and the winds blew and beat against that house, and it fell with a great crash" (Matthew 7:26-27 NIV).

We can hear God speaking with clarity when our priorities are right and when we sincerely desire restoration. He always has something to say to us, but we hear him more clearly when we are ready to obey Him and fight the enemy of our souls.

Like us, the Israelites had to fight their adversaries, but their opponents attempted to slay them with spears and swords. Our enemy is different.

For we do not wrestle against flesh and blood, but against

*principalities, against powers, against the rulers of the darkness
of this age, against spiritual hosts of wickedness in the heavenly
places (Ephesians 6:12 NKJV).*

Because of the battles that the Israelites experienced,
there were times that the temple was in dire need of repair.
One example can be found during the reign of Josiah. (See
2 Kings 22:1-7.) Josiah zealously and aggressively began
cleaning up Jerusalem and Judah by destroying the things
that didn't belong in the lives of God's people. (See 2
Chronicles 34:1-8.) A similar instance can be found in 2
Kings 12:4-5, when King Joash repaired the temple.

As a brief aside, that first magnificent temple was
destroyed by the Babylonians in 586 BC. (See 2 Kings 25:8-
9.) A new temple was eventually built following their return
from captivity in Babylon. (See Ezra 3:7-11.) In AD 70, that
second temple was destroyed by the Romans. Interestingly,
both the first and second temples were destroyed on the
same day of the Jewish Calendar, 656 years apart.[27] At the
time of this writing, the Muslim Al-Aqsa Mosque and Dome
of the Rock stand where the Jewish temple once stood.

As Christians, the fixing that we may need from the
battles we undergo can seem discouraging and endless, but a
dedicated life always has a cost. I'm afraid that in our zealous
approaches to the unsaved, we may have painted unrealistic
pictures of Christian eutopia to potential converts. There is
truly tremendous joy and blessing for those who love God,
but there is more that must be said.

Billy Graham said, "The Christian life is not a constant
high. I have my moments of deep discouragement. I have to
go to God in prayer with tears in my eyes, and say, 'O God,
forgive me,' or 'Help me.'"[28]

*He who overcomes, I will make him a pillar in the temple
of My God, and he shall go out no more. I will write on him the*

name of My God and the name of the city of My God, the New Jerusalem, which comes down out of heaven from My God. And I will write on him My new name (Revelation 3:12 NKJV).

The subject of a third temple to be built in Jerusalem is currently a hot topic, particularly with teachers of eschatology. Many believe that the temple must be constructed before the Messiah returns, but no one knows exactly when this will happen.

The book of Revelation tells us where there will be another, very different temple, and repair will never be needed.

The twelve gates were twelve pearls, each gate a single pearl. The main street of the City was pure gold, translucent as glass. But there was no sign of a Temple, for the Lord God—the Sovereign-Strong—and the Lamb are the temple. The City doesn't need sun or moon for light. God's Glory is its light, the Lamb its lamp! The nations will walk in its light and earth's kings bring in their splendor. Its gates will never be shut by day, and there won't be any night (Revelation 21:21-25 MSG).

Heart Hygiene
Questions for
Chapter 13

1. When something needs repair, tools are usually needed. What "tools" can you use when your "house" needs repair?

2. Read Psalm 34:18 and describe the sort of person to whom the Lord draws near and rescues.

3. In 2 Chronicles 34:1-8, King Josiah purged Judah and Jerusalem before the temple was repaired. Why do you think the clean-up of the nation was necessary before the restoration of the building?

4. God gave a specific plan for the building of the temple in Jerusalem. Share some personal directive or correction that God has given for building the "house of you."

5. Explain some of the battles that we all have in various personal daily "wars" that might exhaust us and make us desperate for renewal. (See Ephesians 6:12.)

6. Read James 4:1. What could be a reason we need repairs?

7. According to Matthew 7:26-27, why is it important to keep the "house of you" in good repair?

FOURTEEN

Arsenal Supply

*The **LORD** has opened his armory and brought out weapons to vent his fury. The terror that falls upon the Babylonians will be the work of the Sovereign **LORD** of Heaven's Armies (Jeremiah 50:25 NLT).*

Babylon, both literal and mystical, has been recognized as the traditional enemy of God's truth and His people.[29] In the book of Revelation, Babylon is a symbol of apostacy and those principles which deny the truth. Someday soon, Heaven's Armies will destroy this Babylon that has been opposing righteousness and led many astray from the beginning of time. (See Revelation 18). Until that day, the children of God must continue to resist their hostile adversary, but the only way to do that is through the power of God.

Submit therefore to God. Resist the devil and he will flee from you (James 4:7 NASB).

Jesus taught us effective ways to resist the Devil by His example. One example is found in Matthew 4:1-11, when the Lord fasted 40 days and 40 nights. After all that time without food, He was terribly hungry.

Doctors assert that some standard medical tests require that their patients must go without food a certain amount of time before the testing is done. Going without eating a single thing, even for one day, is not a comfortable thing for us to do. Our stomachs growl, and the thought of food makes our mouths water with longing. Even if we aren't especially hungry, thinking about certain foods can start us craving them.

Fasting requires a lot of self-discipline, but Jesus taught us that in our fight of resisting the Devil, there is purpose in giving up food for a period of time. Fasting is a weapon that can break the power of our enemy.

For the weapons of our warfare are not carnal but mighty in God for pulling down strongholds . . . (2 Corinthians 10:4 NKJV).

Among other things, when we use the "ammunition" of fasting, it can help to bring us clarity and direction. Both fasting and prayer can help in uncluttering our worldliness as we prioritize the things of the Spirit. Nineteenth-century author Andrew Murray once said, "Prayer is reaching out after the unseen; fasting is letting go of all that is seen and temporal."[30]

"Is not this the kind of fasting I have chosen: to loose the chains of injustice and untie the cords of the yoke, to set the oppressed free and break every yoke? Is it not to share your food with the hungry and to provide the poor wanderer with shelter— when you see the naked, to clothe them, and not to turn away from your own flesh and blood? Then your light will break forth like the dawn, and your healing will quickly appear; then your righteousness will go before you, and the glory of the LORD will be your rear guard" (Isaiah 58:6-8 NIV).

After Jesus had been fasting for 40 days and nights, the Devil first tempted Him with food. If you've had any experience with fasting, or perhaps dieting for weight loss, you know the agony of resisting food when you're hungry. Those days of fasting were not easy for Jesus either, but He showed us how we can respond when tempted.

But He answered and said, "It is written, 'Man shall not live by bread alone, but by every word that proceeds from the mouth of God.'" (Matthew 4:4 NKJV).

Satan tried to tempt Jesus in other ways, but each time, Jesus responded with the Word of God, and the Devil left Him. The Lord fought the enemy with the sword of the Spirit (see Ephesians 6:17), a most effective weapon. He showed us how to arm ourselves with scripture verses to keep us from being slain.

For the word of God is living and powerful, and sharper than any two-edged sword, piercing even to the division of soul and spirit, and of joints and marrow, and is a discerner of the thoughts and intents of the heart (Hebrews 4:12 NKJV).

The Bible indicates that there is a *time for war.* (See Ecclesiastes 3:8.) It won't always be with guns, bombs, or manmade artillery, but there surely will be battles.

. . . I see a different law in the members of my body, waging war against the law of my mind and making me a prisoner of the law of sin which is in my members (Romans 7:23 NASB).

In the bestselling book, *Battlefield of the Mind*, Joyce Meyer explains, "Through careful strategy and cunning deceit, Satan attempts to set up 'strongholds' in our mind."[31] However, we can choose to take our thoughts captive (see 2 Corinthians 10:5) and fight with our faith.

Fight the good fight of faith; take hold of the eternal life to which you were called, and you made the good confession in the presence of many witnesses (1 Timothy 6:12 NASB).

Our good confession is also a valuable weapon to use in our battle against evil. In fact, all the words we think or speak will influence the outcome. Positive, truthful words are extremely valuable in our fight.

On the other hand, when we speak negatively, we are foolishly submitting to our foe. We give the Devil power when we entertain his lies. Furthermore, if our behavior is lazy, passive or disobedient in any way, the enemy gains strongholds. If we haven't studied the Bible, we'll lack the knowledge for applying God's Word and truth. Being ignorant of the Word will make us less victorious, but if we know the Word, we are reassured.

Though an army besiege me, my heart will not fear; though war break out against me, even then I will be confident (Psalm 27:3 NIV).

We have been given enough weapons to fight and win the battle. Among other mighty defenses, we have praise and worship, love, forgiveness, and joy. Our ultimate help and rescue are found in the very name of JESUS! There is unsurpassed power in the name of Jesus Christ.

When our time on this earth ends and we stand before His glorious presence, may we be able to say, along with Paul, *"I have fought the good fight, I have finished the race, I have kept the faith"* (2 Timothy 4:7 NKJV).

God has provided us with the arsenal that can literally save our lives. Most of our weapons are invisible to the eye, but they are more powerful than any armament that could be manufactured. We can wield them as soon as the enemy appears.

So take everything the Master has set out for you, well-made weapons of the best materials. And put them to use so you will be able to stand up to everything the Devil throws your way. This is no afternoon athletic contest that we'll walk away from and forget about in a couple of hours. This is for keeps, a life-or-death fight to the finish against the Devil and all his angels (Ephesians 6:11-12 MSG).

Heart Hygiene
Questions for
Chapter 14

1. Read Matthew 4:1-11 and list the things with which the Devil tried to tempt Jesus.

2. What weapon is mentioned in 2 Corinthians 6:7?

3. According to Psalm 149:4, who gets victory?

4. If you have fasted successfully, explain what you think it did for you and can do for others.

5. How can we overcome the world? (See 1 John 5:4.)

6. Give an example of how changing your mind can be an effective weapon.

7. Read Ephesians 6:13-17. Beginning with verse 14, list the articles of the armor.

FIFTEEN

Joy in the House

Rejoice in the Lord always; again, I will say, rejoice! (Philippians 4:4 NASB).

Have you ever been in a busy shopping mall, or in a traffic jam, or somewhere where there are people coming and going, where you could carefully observe the general expression on their faces? When I've done that lately, I've noticed that there aren't many smiles. In fact, overall, a lot of the people I've observed in crowds don't have a happy countenance.

Look at that verse in Philippians 4:4 again. Can't you just hear Paul enthusiastically repeating the phrase? **"Rejoice! Again, I say, 'Rejoice!'"** Maybe he was also looking at some gloomy faces in the crowds and trying to encourage them.

A cheerful heart is good medicine, but a crushed spirit dries up the bones (Proverbs 17:22 NIV).

As a side note, I've had the experience of playing the piano in front of congregations for worship services in different churches over the years, and I've also stood in front of groups to lead a Bible study. I think music leaders, pastors and teachers can identify with me when I say, it's a little discouraging if you're looking out at uninspired, passive or sleepy faces in the audience. On the other hand, when we see responsive smiles and enthusiasm indicating receptiveness or participation, we are spurred on.

I think it's important to express cheerfulness whenever we can. Unfortunately, there doesn't appear to be many people who have joy, especially in the general public. I've noticed that, more often than not, a blank face is returned when I've attempted to wave, say hello or smile at a passing stranger. Of course, only God can really see what a person is feeling. Sometimes external appearance is deceiving.

Do you remember when the prophet, Samuel, was searching for the right king to choose and anoint for leading the people? As he looked around for the potential leader, God made it clear that He doesn't make choices based on the same things people admire. (See 1 Samuel 16:7.) God's perspective is quite different from ours, because He can see into the heart, and he can see when we're smiling or frowning on the inside.

God is looking at **your** heart. He knows **exactly** what you think and feel at all times. King David understood that fact, and he gave his son good advice in the following verse.

"And you, Solomon my son, get to know well your father's God; serve him with a whole heart and eager mind, for GOD examines every heart and sees through every motive. If you seek him, he'll make sure you find him, but if you abandon him, he'll leave you for good. Look sharp now! GOD has chosen you to build his holy house. Be brave, determined! And do it!" (1 Chronicles 28:9-10 MSG).

Trials and troubles face everyone—I'm afraid it is often apparent on our faces—but it's really not that difficult to wear a smile. Beauty consultants have suggested that simple facial exercises help to keep our faces from wrinkles and will help us look youthful and radiant. I hope it works. As I see it, smiling could be the easiest exercise that I can do.

You've probably heard people say it's important to "Dress for success." One's attire might help a person to present a positive image, but I'm convinced that the responsive expressions on our faces leave a longer-lasting impression than Dior or Armani. Not only can a smile touch the heart of the person you may be smiling at, it does something for you, too.

According to scientists, "When our smiling muscles contract, they fire a signal back to the brain, stimulating our reward system, and further increasing our level of happy hormones, or endorphins. In short, when our brain feels happy, we smile; when we smile, our brain feels happier."[32] Experiment with this principle to evaluate if you do indeed feel something. Make it a point to purposely smile more today.

Like Hannah in Old Testament times, we can practice smiling. Also, like her, we even have reason to smile at our enemies.

And Hannah prayed and said: "My heart rejoices in the LORD; My horn is exalted in the LORD. I smile at my enemies, Because I rejoice in Your salvation" (1 Samuel 2:1 NKJV).

The Word of God brings joy. If you need a little motivation to put a grin on your face and joy in your heart, open the Bible and read. There are happy stories of victory and rescue. Read about how David defeated Goliath with a mere slingshot, or about Noah's ark and the first rainbow, and there's a whale of a story in Jonah.

The statutes of the LORD are right, rejoicing the heart; The commandment of the LORD is pure, enlightening the eyes (Psalm 19:8 NKJV).

There is another way to have joy (or the opposite) that

is often overlooked. We can smile with our mouth, but even more importantly is what we speak with our mouth. (See Matthew 12:37.) Our lives have been affected by every word we've spoken since the day we were born.[33] Like the following verses, the book of Proverbs brings repeated advice regarding the significance of our talking.

A man has joy in an apt answer, And how delightful is a timely word! (Proverbs 15:23 NASB).

Death and life are in the power of the tongue, And those who love it will eat its fruit (Proverbs 18:21 NKJV).

Too much talk leads to sin. Be sensible and keep your mouth shut (Proverbs 10:19 NLT).

Words satisfy the mind as much as fruit does the stomach; good talk is as gratifying as a good harvest (Proverbs 18:20 MSG).

Our thoughts and words can be a source of happiness, but sometimes it seems there is no rhyme or reason for why we feel grumpy or discontented. When that happens, it may be a good idea to review what we have been speaking and thinking. If our words or thoughts are negative (i.e., complaining, selfish, slanderous, etc.), they will steal our joy.

On the other hand, a thankful heart is a joyful heart. Someone said, "It is not happy people who are thankful, it is thankful people who are happy."[34] Interestingly, individuals who are grateful are the most contented, and they are also the most enjoyable people with whom we associate. May God give each of us a spirit of true thanksgiving!

I know that there is nothing better for people than to be happy and to do good while they live. That each of them may eat and drink, and find satisfaction in all their toil—this is the gift of God (Ecclesiastes 3:12-13 NIV).

A "house" with laughter can actually reduce pain, according to some people. Norman Cousins, who suffered from degenerative collagen disease, wrote about "Laugh

Therapy" in his book, *Anatomy of An Illness*. He said, "The joyous discovery of ten minutes of genuine belly laughter had an anesthetic effect and would give me at least two hours of painless sleep."[35]

If laughter can lessen pain, it stands to reason that sadness could have the opposite effect. So, I suspect that people who have a good sense of humor probably have an advantage in overcoming suffering.

When the righteous see God in action they'll laugh, they'll sing, they'll laugh and sing for joy (Psalm 68:3 MSG).

Heart Hygiene
Questions for
Chapter 15

1. Read Deuteronomy 28:47-48. The Israelites were warned what would happen to them if they disobeyed. Why was it important for them to serve God with joy, and why is it still important for us today?

2. Nehemiah said, ". . . *the joy of the LORD, is your strength.*" (See Nehemiah 8:10 NASB.) Relate a time when you felt strong in the Spirit of God despite difficult circumstances in your life.

3. Children have been taught not to speak to strangers. Some adults won't respond to strangers for similar (cautionary) reasons. In your opinion, when is it acceptable or unacceptable to greet strangers?

4. Read Ecclesiastes 5:18-20. There are some people who are very rich, but they don't have joy. Do you think that some people are happier than others, even though they may have less possessions? If so, why?

5. According to 1 Peter 1:6, we can rejoice despite our difficulties. Consider something that has caused you to suffer. Then, because we know that God works all things for our good (see Romans 8:28), try to write a sentence or two expressing thanksgiving for whatever it was that was painful.

6. Rate your happiness on a scale of 1-10 with ten being extremely joyful and one being rather sad. Do you have more joy today than you did a few years ago? Why or why not?

7. List three or more things in your life that give you joy.

SIXTEEN

Houseguests

No one who practices deceit will dwell in my house; no one who speaks falsely will stand in my presence (Psalm 101:7 NIV).

It's clear that the Psalmist King David was determined to use carefulness in choosing the people with whom he would associate. He knew that linking up with wicked people would rub off on his life.

Do not be deceived: "Bad company corrupts good morals" (1 Corinthians 15:33 NASB).

Colin Powell wisely said, "The simple but true fact of life is that you become like those with whom you closely associate—for the good and the bad."[36]

Before we go further with this subject, it's important to point out that in attempts to keep ourselves from sinful associations and relationships, we don't actually segregate ourselves from sinful people (i.e., the human race).

"The Son of Man came eating and drinking, and they say, 'Look, a glutton and a winebibber, a friend of tax collectors and sinners!' But wisdom is justified by her children" (Matthew 11:19 NKJV).

Jesus was criticized, yet He treated not only the saints

but all people with love. Likewise, Christians are not to be selective in showing kindness. Isolating ourselves from the heathen would be illogical, since it is our duty to help convert the lost. (See Matthew 16:15.) Rather, the warning that we must heed pertains to avoiding partnering or uniting with anyone that would entice us to do evil.

Do not be bound together with unbelievers; for what partnership have righteousness and lawlessness, or what fellowship has light with darkness? (2 Corinthians 6:14 NASB).

The Israelites were severely cautioned regarding any person who might turn them away from obedience to the Lord. Listen to Moses' stern warning:

"If your brother, the son of your mother, your son or your daughter, the wife of your bosom, or your friend who is as your own soul, secretly entices you, saying, 'Let us go and serve other gods,' which you have not known, neither you nor your fathers, of the gods of the people which are all around you, near to you or far off from you, from one end of the earth to the other end of the earth, you shall not consent to him or listen to him, nor shall your eye pity him, nor shall you spare him or conceal him; but you shall surely kill him; your hand shall be first against him to put him to death, and afterward the hand of all the people. And you shall stone him with stones until he dies, because he sought to entice you away from the LORD your God, who brought you out of the land of Egypt, from the house of bondage. So all Israel shall hear and fear, and not again do such wickedness as this among you" (Deuteronomy 13:6-11 NKJV).

In Old Testament times, the Israelites lived strictly under the law. There was no tolerance for apostasy in any form. Those who turned from God or tried to lead others away from Him were stoned to death. I don't know about you, but I'm very glad for God's mercy toward me.

For the law was given through Moses, but grace and truth came through Jesus Christ (John 1:17 NKJV).

Fortunately, we weren't "*stoned with stones*" when we turned away from God or made friends with the world, or I think we'd *all* be in trouble. However, death is always the result of refusal to obey and submit to God. (See Romans 6:23.)

You adulterous people, don't you know that friendship with the world means enmity against God? Therefore, anyone who chooses to be a friend of the world becomes an enemy of God (James 4:4 NIV).

I don't want to become so comfortable in God's grace that I become careless in my relationships and forget the danger of continued fraternization with bad company. We have been warned that immoral companions will leave negative impressions on our lives. Their influence, even after we pulled away from them, can be compared to a wound, although it may be small, which leaves a scar that doesn't go away.

And now I make one more appeal, my dear brothers and sisters. Watch out for people who cause divisions and upset people's faith by teaching things contrary to what you have been taught. Stay away from them (Romans 16:17 NLT).

The contagion of wickedness will infect and pollute a person's good intentions. Furthermore, it can quickly spread from one individual to another, worse than a virus.

He who keeps the commandment keeps his soul, But he who is careless of conduct will die (Proverbs 19:16 NASB).

Individuals with whom we interact the most frequently normally exert the most influence in our lives. Surrounding ourselves with family, friends and leaders who have wisdom and integrity will help us to absorb good things instead of negatives.

I am a friend to all who fear you, to all who follow your precepts (Psalm 119:63 NIV).

It is profitable for Christians to meet regularly together. It's not just a religious legality without benefits. Among other things, we refine each other.

Iron sharpens iron, So one man sharpens another (Proverbs 27:17 NASB).

Christian fellowship is an opportunity for us to inspire one another, and we are spurred on by encouragement. As we do good things together, we experience power in our unity.

Let us think of ways to motivate one another to acts of love and good works. And let us not neglect our meeting together, as some people do, but encourage one another, especially now that the day of his return is drawing near (Hebrews 10:24-25 NLT).

We may have many kinds of friends. Our "best" friend might be someone we've known for a long or a short time. We have friends that we don't know in settings other than the place we always see them. That might be in the workplace, the gym, or church, for instance. We have childhood friends that will always be considered friends–even though our lives may have taken different directions. We may also have family friends, social media friends, neighbor friends, business friends, political friends, fancy friends, young friends, noisy friends, funny friends, and more.

Jesus taught us another class of people to befriend. He told us to invite them to be our houseguests.

Then he turned to the host. "The next time you put on a dinner, don't just invite your friends and family and rich neighbors, the kind of people who will return the favor. Invite some people who never get invited out, the misfits from the wrong side of the tracks. You'll be—and experience—a blessing. They won't be able to return the favor, but the favor will be returned—oh, how it will be returned!—at the resurrection of God's people" (Luke 14:12-14 MSG).

As a child, I remember learning an old song with the words, "Make new friends, and keep the old. One is silver and the other gold." Having good friends is actually better than having silver or gold, and our most valuable friend, Jesus Christ, is priceless. He is our eternal friend, past, present and future. He always has been, and always will be, the best friend possible.

And the scripture was fulfilled that says, "Abraham believed God, and it was credited to him as righteousness," and he was called God's friend (James 2:23 NIV).

Whenever we feel lonely, we know that the friendship of Jesus is always available to us with His love and comfort. Remember: Jesus said. ". . . I am with you always . . ." (Matthew 28:20 NIV).

One day, when I was telling the Lord that I was feeling lonely, He showed me that loneliness has a cure. I learned that often the epitome of loneliness is due to SELF-ishness. Whenever I turned inward, feeling sorry for myself, and especially when I felt unsatisfied or bored, I was opening the door for loneliness. With a little effort, however, I could change my mind by concentrating on someone other than myself. I found that even a simple communication to another person can alleviate loneliness—just by being a friend and focusing on my friend instead of on me. Jesus taught us what that means by His example.

This is how we know what love is: Jesus Christ laid down his life for us. And we ought to lay down our lives for our brothers and sisters (1 John 3:16 NIV).

Heart Hygiene
Questions for
Chapter 16

1. Name 3-5 people (not necessarily your best friends) with whom you usually spend the most time each week.

2. Read Proverbs 18:24. What are some qualities of a great friend?

3. List the names of a few individuals who you think have influenced your life in a positive way. (Examples: teachers, leaders, neighbors, family members, etc.)

4. Explain what you think "*friendship with the world*" means. (See James 4:4.)

5. Read Proverbs 27:6. Have you experienced pain from a friend's words, even though he or she was truthful? If so, explain what that has meant to you.

6. Since *"Bad company corrupts good morals"* (*1 Corinthians 15:33 NASB*), describe what you think *bad company* implies.

7. What does 2 Corinthians 6:14 mean to you?

SEVENTEEN

House Security

For he will command his angels concerning you to guard you in all your ways (Psalm 91:11 NIV).

It seems like a lot of the houses and vehicles in our neighborhoods have security systems. Alarms will go off when someone tries to break into them. Actually, as you are probably well aware, they go off at other times, too. I've thought that the sound of that horrendous ringing wasn't that effective for alerting the police, since alarm noise was present *somewhere* all the time. I think everyone sort of became desensitized to it.

There's another kind of alarm system to which people may become dangerously desensitized. It is a warning that some call a conscience, but it's more than that. Christians will recognize the alert which I'm referring to as the voice of the Holy Spirit. It's usually not particularly loud or blaring. Nevertheless, it definitely should get our attention.

My sheep hear My voice, and I know them, and they follow Me (John 10:27 NKJV).

We have been advised to carefully and continually watch and listen for the Master. If we are focused on the wrong things, we become oblivious to the cautioning that the Lord provides for our safety. Lives have been ruined because people haven't sought the wisdom and knowledge of God. (See Hosea 4:6.)

"Listen to me, O my people, while I give you stern warnings. O Israel, if you would only listen to me!" (Psalm 81:8 NLT).

I hear the passionate cry of God in that verse, and it deeply touches my heart. If you are a parent, you probably remember begging your child to listen, maybe even shaking the child to pay attention, knowing that he or she could be terribly hurt if he or she did not learn what you were trying to teach. Try to feel the broken heart that Jesus must have had.

"O Jerusalem, Jerusalem, the one who kills the prophets and stones those who are sent to her! How often I wanted to gather your children together, as a hen gathers her chicks under her wings, but you were not willing!" (Matthew 23:37 NKJV).

The Lord has our safety in mind. If a house has a burglar alarm that isn't connected to the power source, it won't be set off to signal the homeowners of an intruder. It must be connected for it to be heard and to be useful for security. Similarly, we need to be united with the Holy Spirit for the power that keeps us safe and alerts us to danger.

If we live in the Spirit, let us also walk in the Spirit (Galatians 5:25 NKJV).

The Lord has explicit directions for us. Those priceless guidelines, which assure us of peace, well-being, prosperity, health and safety, are clearly pointed out in the Bible, but until they are acknowledged and read and studied, the connection isn't made. Like the disconnected burglar alarm, we remain vulnerable to intruders if we don't know God's Word. On the other hand, actively looking for the truth and abiding in the Holy Spirit is always the safest place to be.

But let all who take refuge in you be glad; let them ever sing for joy. Spread your protection over them, that those who love your name may rejoice in you (Psalm 5:11 NIV).

Good protection depends on our obedience. It is those who *take refuge* in the Lord, that have guaranteed protection. In chapter 14, "Arsenal Supply," the subject pertained to preparing for our part in the warfare, just as Paul advised Timothy.

Timothy, my son, I am giving you this command in keeping with the prophecies once made about you, so that by recalling them you may fight the battle well (1 Timothy 1:18 NIV).

As we fight, we may become exhausted in building our various fortifications to keep our "house" secure. The housebreakers, the devil and his demons, bombard and tempt us continually. We need to do what we can to fight and resist our enemy to help maintain security, but ultimately, the battle is the Lord's (see 1 Samuel 17:47). Our security is always dependent on Him.

You are from God, little children, and have overcome them; because greater is He who is in you than he who is in the world (1 John 4:4 NASB).

Our enemies are always trying to break in and destroy our peace, but He who lives in us has a lot more power! Compared to Almighty God, Satan is much less than a pesky mosquito.

Say to God, "How awesome are your deeds! Your enemies cringe before your mighty power" (Psalm 66:3 NLT).

Jesus taught us to pray, ". . . *deliver us from evil"* (Matthew 6:13 KJV). God is our Deliverer, but He may wait on bringing His deliverance until we do our part. (See Ephesians 6:13.) We are not puppets, and because we have the option of choosing right or wrong, we must give a righteous response to situations that threaten our safety by doing, thinking and speaking what is right. Common sense is a valuable security feature in helping to keep us safe. As we trust God and step out in obedience, His mighty rescue power is activated.

The Lord will rescue me from every evil attack and will bring me safely to his heavenly kingdom. To him be glory for ever and ever. Amen (2 Timothy 4:18 NIV).

The subject of our "house" security and protective needs referred to up to this point have pertained to our soul and spirit, but the safety of our physical body is also important. We see media reports indicating widespread criminal activity and violence, including theft, assault, murder, torture, and rape, to mention a few unfortunately common occurrences in the world. The underlying cause of hatred always stems from Satanic motivation, but like our spiritual need for care, we must use wisdom and deal cautiously with the physical world.

When you were growing up, a parent may have said to you when you left the house, "Stay out of trouble!" You knew exactly what that meant without further elaboration. They wanted you to avoid bad environments, troublemakers and foolishness of any kind.

You also may have heard, "Don't drink, smoke or chew, or go with those who do." It may sound laughable or a little legalistic, but those words were used as a reminder for us to make an effort to be pure.

Keep your eyes open, hold tight to your convictions, give it all you've got, be resolute, and love without stopping (1 Corinthians 16:13-14 MSG).

To help in keeping our physical bodies from jeopardy, it is important to stay away from anything that already has a reputation for trouble. Yet, it's more than rowdy bars and dark alleys that should be sidestepped. It might be a club or organization without Christian ideals. It may be accepting invitations to parties where people don't have good ethics. Remember that physical problems can often stem from bad attitudes, and we know that even poor thinking can be contagious.

Hear my voice, O God, in my complaint; Preserve my life from dread of the enemy. Hide me from the secret counsel of evildoers, From the tumult of those who do iniquity (Psalm 64:1-2 NASB).

Studies have shown us that there is a mind-body connection. For instance, doctors have indicated that stress will cause various ailments. A growing body of research suggests that negative emotions and thoughts may also have links to other serious health problems, like heart disease.[37]

There is much more that could be said regarding the current studies of the mind-body connection, but the Bible has contained information on that subject all along.

*And you shall love the **LORD** your God with all your heart, with all your soul, with all your mind, and with all your strength. This is the first commandment (Mark 12:30 NKJV).*

The Lord is our ultimate protector and Savior as we abide in Him.

You are my hiding place; you will protect me from trouble and surround me with songs of deliverance (Psalm 32:7 NIV).

Heart Hygiene
Questions for
Chapter 17

1. List five things mentioned in Romans 8:38-39 that cannot separate us from the love of God.

2. What were the conditions expected of the Israelites in order to be protected and delivered from their enemies, as noted in Deuteronomy 23:14?

3. Read Psalm 31:4, then name at least one type of "trap" of the enemy.

4. Tell of a personal "warning" from the Lord that you could share with others today.

5. Give a specific example of an incident when you knew that God protected or delivered you from danger.

6. Is there an evil you want God to deliver you from today, and what is your part in this deliverance?

7. What area of your life have you felt the most vulnerable (or unsafe), and was it physically or spiritually that you were troubled? (See Psalm 20:1.)

EIGHTEEN

What's Cookin'?

"I the LORD *search the heart and examine the mind, to reward each person according to their conduct, according to what their deeds deserve" (Jeremiah 17:10 NIV).*

Sometimes when my husband comes home from work in the evening, the first thing that comes out of his mouth is, "What's cookin'?" His question might not merely be insinuating that he wants a description of what's on the stove or in the oven, but usually, it *does* pertain to the meal I'm preparing for his supper.

I try to cook dinners that are nutritious for us, but sometimes I would prefer to eat nothing but chocolate. Of course, an everyday diet of nothing but chocolate would eventually kill me. In the same way, I can choose what I put in my mind, whether it's healthy or not, but a continual diet of wrong thinking could also kill me.

In previous chapters, I have already said a lot about what we allow into our minds and the fact that our thinking can affect our body, soul and spirit, both positively and negatively. I even wrote an entire book about the influence of our thoughts and our words[38], but I continue to find it to be an inexhaustible subject from which we can learn.

Many kinds of thoughts travel through our brains continually. Sometimes, "what's cookin'" in our minds and hearts may have more relevance than at other times, depending on the origin. We can be fired up with a peaceful, Godly flame that inspires our thoughts, or it can be that horrid, destructive fire of Hell that causes devastation.

Examine me, O LORD, and try me; Test my mind and my heart (Psalm 26:2 NASB).

The source of our thoughts is significant to how they will manifest. Good or bad, they will certainly produce—if they remain. For instance, if they came from an impure source, and they are not rejected, they will surely yield unpleasantness.

Don't be misled: No one makes a fool of God. What a person plants, he will harvest. The person who plants selfishness, ignoring the needs of others—ignoring God!— harvests a crop of weeds. All he'll have to show for his life is weeds! But the one who plants in response to God, letting God's Spirit do the growth work in him, harvests a crop of real life, eternal life (Galatians 6:7-8 MSG).

Not only must we be cautious with our words, we need to be careful about what we "plant" in our mind, because our thoughts produce words. Maybe you've had someone tell you, "You think too much." Although we have the power to *change* our minds, I don't think we can purposely, completely, turn off all our thinking, even though there may be times we'd like to stop certain thoughts.

For their hearts are like an oven As they approach their plotting; Their anger smolders all night, In the morning it burns like a flaming fire (Hosea 7:6 NASB).

Steve Taylor, Ph.D., senior lecturer in psychology at Leeds Beckett University said, "Our mind is filled with the chaos of swirling thoughts that we have little or no control over."[39] The Apostle Paul confessed that he had similar trouble.

What I don't understand about myself is that I decide one way, but then I act another, doing things I absolutely despise (Romans 7:15 MSG).

Have you ever wished you could take back your words? I think we've all had times when things fly out of our mouths before we hardly think, causing us embarrassment and regret. The damage has been done, and it is a bitter thing to reap the thoughtless words we have sown.

I'll never forget the trouble, the utter lostness, the taste of ashes, the poison I've swallowed. I remember it all—oh, how well I remember—the feeling of hitting the bottom. But there's one other thing I remember, and remembering, I keep a grip on hope: GOD's loyal love couldn't have run out, his merciful love couldn't have dried up. They're created new every morning. How great your faithfulness! (Lamentations 3:19-23 MSG).

The key to avoiding the desolation of shame and disappointment because of our thoughts and words is by listening for God's guidance ahead of time. Just as He plainly led the Israelites, day and night through the desert (see Psalm 78:14), He is willing to lead us. Although we aren't led as they were by a cloud by day and fire by night, we have the Bible to show the perfect way. For instance, scripture teaches us precautionary measures for our thinking.

It's interesting that the Bible refers to "*the helmet of salvation.*" (See Ephesians 6:17.) We know that when a helmet is worn on the head, it protects the brain. So, it seems that this verse infers that our salvation safeguards our thinking. Most versions of that verse advise us to "*take*" the helmet, and other versions instruct us to "*Put on*" the helmet, but with either wording, we conclude there is action required by us in order to benefit from this safety measure. People who have not been saved don't have that helmet and are much more vulnerable to the enemy.

But people who aren't spiritual can't receive these truths from God's Spirit. It all sounds foolish to them and they can't understand it, for only those who are spiritual can understand what the Spirit means. Those who are spiritual can evaluate all things, but they themselves cannot be evaluated by others. For, "Who can know the LORD's thoughts? Who knows enough to teach him?" But we understand these things, for we have the mind of Christ (1 Corinthians 2:14-16 NLT).

I imagine it might sound self-righteous to some if we said, along with the Apostle Paul, *"we have the mind of Christ,"* but it is possible for every Christian to have the mind of Christ. However, that can't happen unless our minds are governed by the Spirit. (See Romans 8:6.) Furthermore, Paul told us everything that does not come from faith is sin. (See Romans 14:23.)

When we start doubting God or lose our focus, our flesh becomes ruler of our thinking, and our hearts are drawn to worldly things. It's impossible to have the mind of Christ and the mind of the world at the same time. Jesus said we can't serve two masters. (See Luke 16:13.) Jesus must be Lord of all.

"And you must love the LORD your God with all your heart, all your soul, all your mind, and all your strength. The second is equally important: 'Love your neighbor as yourself.' No other commandment is greater than these" (Mark 12:30-31 NLT).

We need to remember that the second part of that commandment is quite connected with the first part. There are times when we may find it seems easier to love the Lord, than it is to love our neighbor, but those two commandments are inseparable. We really don't love God—or love our neighbor—successfully without loving both. The Holy Spirit will bring conviction if we allow hostility for a person to remain in our minds.

I have a serious concern to bring up with you, my friends, using the authority of Jesus, our Master. I'll put it as urgently as I can: you must get along with each other. You must learn to be considerate of one another, cultivating a life in common (1 Corinthians 1:10 MSG).

Knowing that He would soon be arrested and facing His death sentence for us, Jesus prayed for our unity. His prayer request was undoubtedly a high priority for us since He knew what was ahead. Truly, He wants us to see the supreme importance of love and unity.

I am in them and you are in me. May they experience such perfect unity that the world will know that you sent me and that you love them as much as you love me (John 17:23 NLT).

It is not as common as it should be, but when Christians gather in unity with their minds on Jesus, it is one of the most joyful experiences we can have on this earth. When Christ returns, we will at last have perfect unity and nothing will ever again disturb our thinking. (See Ephesians 4:13.) Meanwhile, we can submit our minds to Him.

Set your mind on the things above, not on the things that are on earth. For you have died and your life is hidden with Christ in God (Colossians 3:2-3 NASB).

The Bible tells us of a dreadful day, for those who refuse to submit. Something else will be "cookin'". It seems that most people don't like hearing about it. Nonetheless, it is a fact, and everyone should be warned.

"For behold, the day is coming, Burning like an oven, And all the proud, yes, all who do wickedly will be stubble. And the day which is coming shall burn them up," Says the LORD of

hosts, "That will leave them neither root nor branch" (Malachi 4:1 NKJV).

This fire will not be for those who are God's building (see 1 Corinthians 3:9), but only for those who have refused to receive Jesus Christ, trust in Him and apply the Word of God to their lives. God's people will be tried by a different kind of fire (see 1 Corinthians 3:10-15).

Let the wicked forsake his way, And the unrighteous man his thoughts; And let him return to the LORD, And He will have compassion on him; And to our God, For He will abundantly pardon (Isaiah 55:7 NASB).

Heart Hygiene
Questions for
Chapter 18

1. Read Romans 15:5, then list at least three attitudes of mind which Jesus demonstrated for us.

2. According to John 17:23, how will the world know that God loves His people?

3. What kind of mind has God given us? (See 2 Timothy 1:7.)

4. In the 5th chapter of Galatians, Paul shows what it means to live in freedom versus living in bondage. Give an example of "leaven" we should not allow into our minds (see v. 9).

5. In Matthew 21:28-32, which son in the parable changed his mind and did the right thing?

6. Read Philippians 2:3. Give an example of applying this principle.

7. Write a short prayer asking for God's help to keep you from being deceived.

NINETEEN

Servants

Technically, we should be servants in our own "house," since it is God's building. The Bible tells us to live as God's slaves (see 1 Peter 2:16), to serve the Lord (see Psalm 2:11), to work heartily (see Colossians 3:23), to serve others faithfully (see 1 Peter 4:10), and to do all this with an attitude of humility (see Galatians 5:13), not legalistically, but in the Spirit (see Romans 7:6).

"And if it seems evil to you to serve the LORD, choose for yourselves this day whom you will serve, whether the gods which your fathers served that were on the other side of the River, or the gods of the Amorites, in whose land you dwell. But as for me and my house, we will serve the LORD" (Joshua 24:15 NKJV).

Just as the Israelites did in Old Testament times, we must make up our minds. I've emphasized this statement in different ways repeatedly throughout this book, but if you have made it to this last chapter, I suspect you have made the right decision, because you probably would have dumped this book already if you had decided not to be a servant of the Lord. Conviction, not to mention servanthood, is something that an unrepentant, self-sufficient person simply won't deal with, and this book has a lot of "finger-pointing" truth, which, incidentally, began in my own mirror.

Therefore, since Christ suffered for us in the flesh, arm yourselves also with the same mind, for he who has suffered in the flesh has ceased from sin, that he no longer should live the rest of his time in the flesh for the lusts of men, but for the will of God. For we have spent enough of our past lifetime in doing the will of the Gentiles--when we walked in lewdness, lusts, drunkenness, revelries, drinking parties, and abominable idolatries (1 Peter 4:1-3 NKJV).

Due to the recent Corona Virus pandemic, we were repeatedly advised to wash our hands. Those emergency pronouncements failed to mention, however, the urgency of washing our hearts, which is where all of our problems really begin.

Purify me from my sins, and I will be clean; wash me, and I will be whiter than snow (Psalm 51:7 NLT).

We live in a fallen world, and every day we see injustice, sickness, discord, natural disasters and various heartaches and pains. Even if we're committed servants, we may become dazed by many troubles to which we are exposed. When this happens, we turn to Bible answers to be renewed and cleansed from the accumulated grime of the world, whether it be from our own doing or something else.

By the grace obtained for us in Jesus Christ through His blood, we are forgiven and cleansed. Then we can serve Him in obedience and shine brighter than a house after a good spring cleaning.

How much more, then, will the blood of Christ, who through the eternal Spirit offered himself unblemished to God, cleanse our consciences from acts that lead to death, so that we may serve the living God (Hebrews 9:14 NIV).

Jesus has made us priests of God. (See Revelation 1:6.)

As priests, we obey His Word, express our praise and thanksgiving, are zealous for good works, and share the Good News with others. Each of us has a unique calling in this servanthood, according to God's perfect plan.

But you are the ones chosen by God, chosen for the high calling of priestly work, chosen to be a holy people, God's instruments to do his work and speak out for him, to tell others of the night-and-day difference he made for you—from nothing to something, from rejected to accepted (1 Peter 2:9-10 MSG).

Being called a priest may seem like a lofty title, but in reality, it implies serving. It is not a job that is necessarily esteemed, but rather it involves humility and subjugation. However, because we get all of our strength and power from God, our work is quite fulfilling—and the burden is light! (See Matthew 11:30.)

There are always some people that will not humble themselves to be a servant. They want to be the master. Jesus is not Lord of their lives. Sadly, their lack of soul and spiritual hygiene, will eventually cause their "house" to deteriorate because of accumulated filth.

*But be sure to fear the **LORD** and serve him faithfully with all your heart; consider what great things he has done for you (1 Samuel 12:24 NIV).*

If Jesus is indeed Lord of our lives, we will get to work for Him. A. J. Russell wrote, "There is no standing still in the Christian life. If there is not progress there is retrogression."[40] It's a dangerous thing to remove our hands from that proverbial plow (see Luke 9:62), for *no one* is exempt from the wrath of God.

For it is time for judgment to begin with the household of God; and if it begins with us first, what will be the outcome for those who do not obey the gospel of God? (1 Peter 4:17 NASB).

God doesn't change. He is still speaking to us. He is

passionately calling out to everyone in this 21st century world to turn and listen to Him. There's a lot of religiosity out there, but by all indications, there are still many people who have not truly bowed in submission to the King of kings and Lord of lords. We've been given direction for rescue many times in the following scripture.

If my people, who are called by my name, will humble themselves and pray and seek my face and turn from their wicked ways, then I will hear from heaven, and I will forgive their sin and will heal their land (2 Chronicles 7:14 NIV).

I will end this book with the reminder that the above verse is addressed to *God's people*, not the entire world. We are the ones that need to turn from wicked ways and get our "houses" in order. That's a little hard for some of us to admit, but the outcome of the future and the healing of ourselves and our country is dependent upon us, God's servants.

Finally, remember that it's not too late to clean up the "house of you." God's grace is still available. I pray that, along with me, you'll do your best to be diligent in your housework, and that God will build each of us a spectacular home in Heaven where we will meet someday soon (see 2 Corinthians 5:1).

Every house has a builder, but the Builder behind them all is God. Moses did a good job in God's house, but it was all servant work, getting things ready for what was to come. Christ as Son is in charge of the house. Now, if we can only keep a firm grip on this bold confidence, we're the house! (Hebrews 3:4-6 MSG).

Heart Hygiene
Questions for
Chapter 19

1. Name at least two attributes of a servant.

2. Name at least one way where God has asked you to serve.

3. What are some things that should be on your priority list to do as a servant?

4. Explain what you think Jesus meant in Luke 9:62.

5. According to Romans 12:11, what is something we need in order to serve well?

6. Read Luke 10:2. Why do you think there are few workers?

7. What is the difference between freely serving and legalistically serving? (See Romans 7:6.)

So then you are no longer strangers and aliens, but you are fellow citizens with the saints, and are of God's household, having been built on the foundation of the apostles and prophets, Christ Jesus Himself being the corner stone, in whom the whole building, being fitted together, is growing into a holy temple in the Lord, in whom you also are being built together into a dwelling of God in the Spirit (Ephesians 2:19-22 NASB).

End Notes

1   The importance of having a firm foundation is seen in Luke 6:47-49.

2   God knew us before our birth, as indicated in Psalm 139:13.

3   See 2 Corinthians 5:1 regarding our new dwelling.

4   Got Questions? Your Questions: Biblical Answers, https://www.gotquestions.org/cleanliness-next-godliness.html

5   *As it is written: There is none righteous, no, not one (Romans 3:10 NKJV).*

6   *Jesus replied, "Very truly I tell you, no one can see the kingdom of God unless they are born again" (John 3:3 NIV).*

7   Habits for Wellbeing–20 Inspirational Quotes on Change, #18, https://www.habitsforwellbeing.com/20-inspirational-quotes-on-change/

8   Quotes Gram—Famous Quotes About Starting Over, https://quotesgram.com/famous-quotes-about-starting-over

9   *Sir Galahad* by Alfred Lord Tennyson (1842), *The International Thesaurus of Quotations*, Purity, p. 523; compiled by Rhoda Thomas Tripp, Harper & Row Publishers, 1987.

10 Medline Plus, Obsessive-Compulsive Disorder (quoted from the Summary section), https://medlineplus.gov/obsessive compulsivedisorder.html

11 *My Utmost For His Highest*, by Oswald Chambers, original edition 1935, by Dodd, Mead & Company.

12 T.S. Eliot, *Religion and Literature*, 1935, Self-Knowledge 868, p. 577; compiled by Rhoda Thomas Tripp, Harper & Row Publishers, 1987.

13 Live Life Happy Blog, https://livelifehappy.com/life-quotes/the-hardest-part-isnt-choosing, 05/14/2012, by Robert Tew.

14 *He Whispers Your Name*, 2016, December 20th devotional by Cherie Hill, Christian Art Publishers ISBN 978-1-4321-1778-8

15 WebMD, https://www.webmd.com/diet/news/20100210/percentage-of-overweight-obese-americans-swells#1

16 Quote Investigator, https://quoteinvestigator.com/2012/07/18/best-not-seen

17 *Reader's Digest*, March 2020, "Get Angry the Right Way," p. 25.

18 "The dark reasons so many rich people are miserable human beings" by Catey Hill, Market Watch, published Feb. 22, 2018, at 8:13 pm. ET, https://www.marketwatch.com/story/the-dark-reasons-so-many-rich-people-are-miserable-human-beings-2018-02-22

19 Forbes Quotes, More Quotes by Ambrose Bierce, https://www.forbes.com/quotes/386/

20 *"In everything I did, I showed you that by this kind of hard work we must help the weak, remembering the words the Lord Jesus himself said: 'It is more blessed to give than to receive'"* (Acts 20:35 NIV).

21 French words for "Joy of Life".

22 "10 Reasons I'm Thankful for Thankfulness" by Christy Wright, https://www.daveramsey.com/blog/10-reasons-im-thankful-for-thankfulness

23 *But if we walk in the light as He is in the light, we have fellowship with one another, and the blood of Jesus Christ His Son cleanses us from all sin* (1 John 1:7 NKJV).

24 *Webster's New College Dictionary*, p. 690, Wiley Publishing, Inc., 2005.

25 John Donne Quotes, Brainy Quote, https://www.brainyquote.com/authors/john-donne-quotes

26 *Reader's Digest*, "Connect with Strangers," p. 21, April 2020.

27 "The Destruction of the Second Temple", http://www.templemount.org/destruct2.html

28 Christian Quotes, Quotes About Discouragement, https://www.christianquotes.info/quotes-by-topic/quotes-about-discouragement

29 Bible Ask, "What does the word Babylon mean?", https://bibleask.org/word-babylon-mean-book-revelation

30 Crosswalk, Devotionals, https://www.first15.org/10/11/seeking-god-through-fasting/

31 *Battlefield of the Mind* by Joyce Meyer, p. 8, ISBN 978-0-446-69109-3

32 British Council, "What's the science behind a smile?", https://www.britishcouncil.org/voices-magazine/famelab-whats-science-behind-smile

33 *HEART WORDS: Considering How Words Impact Our Lives*, Westbow Press, p. xvii, ISBN 978-1-9736-6654-7

34 Author unknown.

35 Healthy Human Blog, "Laughter Therapy: the Surprising Ways Laughter Can Heal", https://waterbottles.healthyhumanlife.com/laughter-therapy-surprising-ways-laughter-can-heal/

36 Goodreads, Colin Powell, Quotes, Quotable Quotes, https://www.goodreads.com/quotes/310930-the-less-you-associate-with-some-people

37 ABC News, "That Bad Attitude May Be Making You Sick", https://abcnews.go.com/Health/bad-attitude-making-sick/story?id=32194211

38 *HEART WORDS: Considering How Words Impact Our Lives*, Westbow Press, p. xvii, ISBN 978-1-9736-6654-7

39 Psychology Today, "Can You Stop Thinking?" by Steve Taylor, Ph.D., https://www.psychologytoday.com/us/blog/out-the-darkness/201503/can-you-stop-thinking

40 *God At Eventide*, p. 76, *Dodd, Mead & Company Inc.,* 1950.

Printed in the United States
By Bookmasters